C000299452

BIG CHIV

DEDICATION

I want to dedicate this book to my family, especially my wife of 34 years, Julia, who has shown unbelievable patience in allowing me to pursue my second love, football, and in doing so has given me so much love and understanding. You have done an incredible job in keeping the family together through good and hard times – you truly are exceptional. You have never ceased to amaze me. You are so versatile that no matter what is put in front of you, you always manage to do it one hundred per cent.

And to Andrea, Melanie, Nick and Luke, who are not only my wonderful children but, along with Julia, my very best friends in life.

BIG CHIV

MY GOALS IN LIFE

by **MARTIN CHIVERS**

with **PAOLO HEWITT**

Published by Vision Sports Publishing in 2009

Vision Sports Publishing
19-23 High Street
London
KT1 1LL

www.visionsp.co.uk

ISBN 13: 978-1905326-74-7

Edited by: Jim Drewett
Copy editing: Ian Turner and Martin Cloake
Design: Doug Cheeseman

Every effort has been made to contact the copyright holders of the photographs used in this book. If there are any errors or omissions, the publishers will be pleased to receive information and will endeavour to rectify any outstanding permissions after publication.

Typeset by Palimpsest Book Production Limited, Grangemouth, Stirlingshire

Printed and bound in the UK by CPI Mackays, Chatham, ME5 8TD

A CIP record for this book is available from the British library

CONTENTS

ACKNOWLEDGEMENTS

MARTIN CHIVERS

I would like to thank all the players from that great Spurs team of the '70s, for without them I would not be writing this book, and of course to our manager, the great man himself, Bill Nicholson, and his assistant Eddie Baily, *for all their kind and understanding words throughout my time with them* . . . Seriously, I see now you really did get the best out of me.

Thanks also to Bill's daughter Jean Bell for allowing me the great honour of looking after her father at official functions, especially his 2004 testimonial.

To Paolo Hewitt, a true Spurs fan whose enthusiasm and persistence month after month eventually got my true feelings down on paper. I want to thank you not only for securing the deal but more importantly for allowing me to show myself in this book.

To my agent Rob Segal, who convinced me that I had a story worth telling and to Jim Drewett who repeatedly pushed Paolo and me for more and in doing so brought out the best in us.

To Norman Dean, who was like a brother to me in those unforgettable early days at Southampton, to Norman Hunter for a wonderful foreword, and to Steve Perryman, Eddie Baily and Alan Mullery for their kind and perceptive words.

To all the Spurs fans whose support and love during my playing career helped me so much that I used to walk out onto that pitch at White Hart Lane feeling ten feet tall, especially those who stood behind the goal at Molineux the night I scored my best ever goal. By my reckoning I have only got about another thousand left to shake hands with.

Talking of which, thanks to Andy Porter, top Spurs historian, for his contributions to this book.

My final thanks go to Tottenham Hotspur Football Club and to all the staff I work with and who make every day I work there an absolute pleasure.

PAOLO HEWITT

I want to thank three people in particular. They are Julia Chivers, whose input and hard work behind the scenes was absolutely invaluable in the making of this book, my editor Jim Drewett, who became my Bill Nicholson and kept telling me to run harder and stop turning my back on the goalkeeper, and Des Hurrion, whose excellence and professionalism in transcribing the tapes is only what you would expect from such a fine old Burbankian. Thanks so much to all three of you.

I want to thank my agent David Luxton who for some reason still supports Leeds but constantly supported me in my desire to complete this mission.

I want to thank all the Spurs fans who helped me throughout this book, especially Nipper, Martin Cloake, Phil Cornwell, Mike Leigh (we will always have Old Trafford!) and Dirty Den.

Lastly, I want to thank the man himself, Martin Chivers, my boyhood idol, who against all of his instincts put so much of himself into this book. In all our meetings I couldn't help but be struck by his immense grace, good nature, humour and humility. They say you should never meet your heroes. You know what?

They are wrong.

FOREWORD

By Norman Hunter

I first came across Martin when he played for Southampton. I remember this big, tall lad hitting the scene and making quite an impact. Martin had everything. He had pace, great touch; he was good in the air, very quick; the only thing he lacked was Joe Jordan's aggression. If he had had that he would have been unstoppable.

Don Revie, my manager at Leeds, would have dossiers on every team and he used to say to us, "Don't leave Chivers alone for one second; guard him all the time because if you don't he will destroy you."

What was amazing about Martin was that he took so much on the pitch from defenders like myself or Jack Charlton yet he never retaliated, not once. In every game he took fearful beatings but he never kicked back.

He was great at Southampton but in that period at Spurs in the early '70s he was unbelievable. He really came into his own then and was probably the best centre forward in the country, if not Europe.

What I like about Martin is that he has the same sort of nature off the field and so I always got on well with him, apart from that 90 minutes when we did battle on the field.

Martin works for Spurs and I work for Leeds and when we were in the Premiership Martin would always look out for me when we came to White Hart Lane. He is a smashing man and I will always wish him the very best.

PROLOGUE

It was 24th October 1970. I was playing for Tottenham Hotspur against Stoke City at White Hart Lane. Up front, of course. A little over two years earlier I had suffered a career-threatening knee injury at the same ground and although I had been back in action for over 12 months, things hadn't been going well. Until that afternoon. For the first time since I had undergone surgery and worked through an excruciating recovery process, I felt I was playing well. Really well.

During the first half, I made myself favourite to get to a loose ball on the halfway line. I shouldered Dennis Smith out of the way, something I thought would please Bill Nicholson, who had been looking for me to be a bit more aggressive on the pitch. That would show him.

With the ball at my feet, I headed towards the Paxton Road end. I knew Smith was chasing me, but I also knew he wasn't going to catch me. Not that day – I had already scored once. I was nearing the penalty area when I saw Gordon Banks coming out of his goal. I looked up and curved the ball right round him, planting it in the back of the net. Perfect. The crowd erupted and I put my hands up above my head to acknowledge their cheers. I never made a great fuss when I scored but this was special. I had proved my doubters wrong. What a feeling.

Coming off the field one or two players had come up and said, "Great goal Chiv, well done." I had used an aggression which Bill hadn't seen before and had cleared a lot of self-doubt away. At 23 I was in the prime of my football career, yet because of my terrible injury I had not been sure if my leg could sustain a heavy tackle. I needed to know – could I give someone a little nudge, could I use my weight, could I get involved in physical contact? I'd proved in that 45 minutes of football that I could and it gave me so much confidence. I came off the pitch really satisfied with myself. There was always a big teapot on a table in the middle of the dressing room so I got my usual cup and sat down. Straight away Bill began snapping at me in front of the whole team. "If you hadn't turned your back on the goalie for that goal kick you could have had a third goal."

Not "Well done, Chiv" or "Great goal". Instead, he laid into me straight away. I thought, "Wait a minute. I have just scored two goals, one of them was fantastic, we are leading 3–0 and we are totally dominant: give us a break." After all, that goal I scored had been something special and everybody knew it.

I didn't say anything back to Bill, I just put my head down. I had never had this experience before. At Southampton Ted Bates would criticise me but he wouldn't hammer me straight away or criticise me in front of everyone else. I felt you should go round the team and tell people face-to-face. You certainly shouldn't single out someone who had just come back from injury and whose confidence is low. I thought, "What do I have to do to satisfy you?"

It was so hard to take. Alan Mullery was sitting to my right and suddenly he stood up. He was the captain and of all the people the captain was the one who could say something. He said, "Now come on Bill, look at him. Don't have a go at him; his head is down. Tell him what he has done well not what he has done wrong."

Bill just looked up and said, "What has it got to do with you? I'm the manager of this team."

Alan said, "I know but he has just scored a fantastic goal out there."

"It has got nothing to do with you," Bill barked back. "I am dealing with this."

And from there the argument got more and more heated. As it did I slipped away to the toilets. That was my get-out. I didn't want to go to the toilet, I just wanted to get in a room away from Bill. Yet even in there, I could still hear the argument raging on. Mullers was shouting. "Just admit you are wrong, Bill, or I'm telling you, you will ruin this player." Bill kept saying,

"I am the manager; this is my job; I know best." The rest of the players all had their heads down or were trying to ignore the argument.

Normally, if there was an argument in the dressing room, it was between the forwards and defence. Often we would come in at half time and if Bill started on at us as a team, the defence – Mike England, Phil Beal, Joe Kinnear, Cyril Knowles – would say, "Well, if those lazy bastards up front would do their bit it would be all right." We would come back with, "Well, if you give goals away like you are giving them away back there . . ."

There was always competition but this was different. This was Bill Nicholson, my manager, having a screaming match with Alan Mullery, my captain. When I came out of the toilet I saw Pat Jennings stand up and rush to get between Bill and Mullers. It honestly looked like the two men were going to start swapping punches. It was unbelievable and totally unexpected, especially when you consider that Bill's record buy is coming back to form and has just scored one of the best goals of his career. My captain and my manager were fighting and I was the cause of it all. I was devastated.

Finally the two men calmed down and we went out for the second half.

It was no surprise that nothing happened in that half. I don't even remember it. Who knows, if he had not spoilt it all for me I could have gone out and scored more. But I didn't. My head was down. It was the first time I realised that Bill was not going to allow my feet to come off the ground. Not by a long shot. Bill didn't want anybody to get above their station and he certainly achieved that on this day.

It was the start of a relationship that would be the most turbulent and volatile that I would ever know as a professional footballer. And I would not have missed it for the world.

CHAPTER ONE

THE KICK-OFF

Ever since I was a little boy scoring goals is all that has ever mattered to me. Nothing else has given me greater satisfaction. Every game I play I have to score. This is why as a young boy I always had a football with me. In the morning before I went to school, I used to kick a ball. I kicked a ball about at lunchtime and, when I came out of school, I would dribble the ball all the way home. With my football I ensured that our garden had no proper plants in it, and that our garden fence, which acted as my goal, was always on the verge of collapse. It wasn't long before I was dreaming about scoring goals. Even in my sleep I was obsessed.

When people see my name they always ask where my middle name 'Harcourt' came from. Well, according to family history, one of my ancestors was a maid to a lord who was a bit of an explorer. When he died on the mountain he was climbing, she told the lady of the manor that she would name her child after him. So 'Harcourt' became part of the Chivers family tree.

My mother, Sidonia, was German. She came to England just after the First World War and settled in Southampton. That was where she met and married my father, Thomas. She was a housewife and he worked on the docks down the road. They were a typical 1940s Southampton couple, who lived at 103 King George's Avenue, Millbrook. I was born on 27th April 1945, just at the end of the War. I have a brother, Tom, seven years older then me, and a sister, Jane, who is seven years younger.

We lived in a three-bedroom semi-detached that stood on a corner. My grandfather had one room, my parents were in another, whilst my brother and I shared the third. To this day, I can't believe two people slept in it. It was little more than a box room but somehow we got two beds and a wardrobe into it. And two six-footers as we got older. Seven years after my birth my sister Jane arrived.

Mum and Dad were Mr and Mrs Roly Poly, short and round. God only knows where my brother and I came from. Physically, we are nothing like them. My dad was a stevedore, a stocky man and very, very strong. After the cranes had unloaded the ships he used these big grappling hooks to haul and then lift the hundredweight loads onto transporters. It kept him fit but it was a tough job.

Southampton was such a big port in those days. I used to love going down to the docks and fishing off one of the piers. Many people in the area worked down there, including my brother and grandfather, or Pop, as we called him. Pop did some clerical work in the offices towards the end of his life and my brother was an electrician at Harland & Wolff next to the docks. Tom was technically very clever and extremely fastidious. He and I were close, but not competitive because of the big age difference. He was never sporty. He played a little cricket but could not kick a ball to save his life.

When I was a kid I was Tom's responsibility and he had to take me everywhere. He hated it. If he went out with some of his friends, I was always tagging along. I think it helped me grow up a bit quicker – I had to keep up with him. We used to go down to a brook at the bottom of the road which was 20 feet wide in places. We used to nick the poles from the allotments and pole vault across the river. It was hair-raising stuff but I did it. In fact, I did everything they did. If they jumped the brook, I jumped the brook. If they climbed a tree, I climbed a tree. I think my desire to keep up with them helped me in later life when I started to play football with guys much older than me.

The streets weren't an aggressive place in those days. There were no gangs of lads going round causing trouble and I certainly never got into a fight. I was more into going to the cinema. We would go on a Saturday morning and exchange American comics outside after the film had finished. Then we would stop at the bakery on the way home and buy a loaf of bread. There was still rationing in place. You had to have coupons to buy anything. My mum always gave me some for myself and sweets were always top of my shopping list. Despite the rationing, we had a good quality of life. We never had a car – we went everywhere on foot or bike – but I have fond memories of those days. Everybody around us was in the same boat and I always remember them as great times.

As I got older, girls would knock at my front door asking for me. Once this girl called Pauline came round and asked, "Is Martin coming out?" I was upstairs and my mum shouted out to me, "Pauline is here and she wants to know if you are going out to play?" I shouted down, "Only if she goes in goal." And she did. She would suffer going in goal just to hang around with me. I used to leather balls at her, smack her in the mouth with them sometimes, but she was a tough girl and she always stayed. We were lucky because the area we played in backed onto the bowling green which had a big high fence so the ball would never go over. We never had to run and get it.

Every year I got a football for Christmas. One year I got a wonderful, brand new leather one. The first time I went down to the recreation ground to play, it bounced over the railings onto the main road and a bloody great big double-decker bus ran over it and burst it. I never did play near the main road again. I went home crying my eyes out but my old man simply went out and got me another ball. He didn't have a lot of money and never spent any on himself, but he was fantastic. Whatever I needed for football, be it boots or a ball – you could play in any old kit – he got it for me. He supported and encouraged me so much in that way. In fact, for Christmas last year I bought my 32-year-old son Nick a pair of football boots. It brought back some great memories and I got a real kick out of following my father's tradition and decking my own son out for football.

My mother was a fantastic support as well. She used to pedal more than two miles on her bike up to the common, where the school team often played, with my sister on the back seat and oranges dangling from the crossbar. She even helped us carry the goalposts. Every time we played she would be there, it didn't matter how far she had to travel.

I spent hours practising my skills but because balls were so heavy in those days you couldn't juggle them for long. Thankfully, plastic balls appeared on the scene and the one great thing about them – apart from saving my dad money – was that you could repair them with a hot iron. All you had to do was melt the plastic and seal over the hole. Mind you, I could never manage to mend the balls myself. Because they were lighter, I could practise with them for hours and challenge myself with targets like trying to keep the ball up with my feet or my head for a hundred times. I never left the rec until I had achieved my target.

Dad was a goalkeeper who had played for Southampton Schoolboys. He must have been in his mid-40s when I started to seriously kick a ball, and although he was busy earning a wage and bringing up a family, I do remember him standing in goal for me a few times. The other person who helped me with football was my German cousin, Hubert, who played in goal for Cologne in Germany. He would come over in the summer and stay with us. I looked forward to his visits because it finally meant I had someone to play with. We would go to the Rec and I would blast balls at him but I never got any past him because he was so good. Still, it was the perfect opportunity for me to practise my shooting and proved very valuable later on.

My primary school was called Foundry Lane. It was a mile up the road from where I lived. There, we used to kick a tennis ball around the playground. If you can dribble with a tennis ball you can dribble with anything. The funny thing is, I was not a football fan, not particularly interested in any team – I just wanted to play. There were a couple of boys from Dr Barnardo's who wore great big hobnail boots. They were real heavy toe-cap things and, shit, you didn't want to get in the way of those. I used to dance round them. Playing football, I wore out the soles of my shoes on a regular basis and once, when I needed new ones, my mum bought me a pair of those hobnail boots because she was pissed off at spending money all the time. Nobody came near me when I had those on.

The person who I remember most from the school was the sports teacher, Mr Melling. He organised the after-school games which I loved. These games were never played on grass: they always took place in the playground of Foundry Lane, which had small goals. It was a restricted area but Mr Melling organised it so well he made it great fun. The only time we did play on grass was when we played matches against other schools. Mr Melling picked that team as well. In those days, we knew nothing about the technical side of football. We didn't know what systems were all about. Back then, you'd have a goalkeeper, you'd have two full backs, three wing halves, two inside forwards, a centre forward and two wingers. Typically you stuck a big man at the back, another at the front and the rest ran round you. A lad called Richard Trimby was six foot one and towered over Mr Melling. He got put at centre half. If anything came at him in the air he did not have to leave the ground, he just headed it away. I was up front.

That primary-school team won a lot of trophies. In one game I scored ten goals against Aldermoor School and the next week in the local paper they ran a cartoon of me. There was a well-known cartoonist, Orf, who worked for the *Southampton Evening Echo* and he drew this cartoon of a goalkeeper saying "Crumbs, this fella Chivers gives me the shivers." I was ten years of age and in the local paper. The school colours were the same red and white as the Southampton team and all through my younger playing days I wore those red-and-white stripes.

In 1958 we got a television at home and the very first thing I remember watching was the famous Real Madrid v Eintracht Frankfurt European Cup final at Hampden Park. It was the best football I had ever seen. The style of football that the likes of Di Stefano and Puskas played that day left me mesmerised. Their skills were unbelievable. Even to this day we know that the continental players have more technical skill than the British players, but watching that team in their all-white strip – which I always loved wearing at Spurs – their skills and passing made an incredible impression on me. The Germans in that game were a terrific team as well. I really felt for their centre forward who scored a hat-trick, only to lose the game.

In the spring of 1956, much to my family's amazement, I passed the 11-plus exam. We had all thought my brother was the brainy one and I was the footballer so it was totally unexpected when the letter confirming my result landed on the doormat. Now I had to make a choice of which grammar school to attend. There were two in Southampton – King Edward's and Taunton's. King Edward's is still there now but it was a rugby school. Taunton's, on the other hand, embraced all sports and had its own playing fields. It was the obvious one for me as it allowed me to continue with my football and also the chance to play regularly on grass.

At Taunton's I started to become something of an all-round sportsman, developing a lot of skills outside of football. I was a good sprinter but I had such a long and laborious stride that no one took me seriously. I was not good at long-distance running but at any distance up to 400 yards I recorded fast times. I had a fair physique with broad shoulders, so I was a natural at throwing. I excelled at the discus and javelin. I played for the Southampton Schools' cricket team and the Hampshire Colts and I went on to be offered the chance to play for Hampshire at cricket. I also represented the school at high jump in the All England Athletics Championships. One thing I wasn't too keen on was swimming. One day the captain of the water polo team, Dave Haller – who later represented England in the Tokyo Olympics – invited me to Jersey to be goalie. Their pool was 30 feet deep, cut out of natural rock, and I spent the 12 minutes each way trying not to drown by hanging onto the crossbar. I only touched the ball twice in a 12–0 win.

But football remained my passion. When I was 14 I was selected for Southampton Schoolboys. The team had some players two years older than me and that gave me great encouragement. I thought if I am playing with these guys I must be good. I played on the wing.

Paul Keeping played in the middle up front. He was taller than me so he could head the ball better than I could, plus he was a bit more aggressive which was never one of my strengths. I didn't go in for hard tackles. My technique was to try and get the ball in front of me so I could run with it and score goals. In that team, I didn't necessarily play a wing game: I just used to stay out of trouble.

I remember the boots I had. They were these high-ankled ones, made of real leather with hard toe-caps, although not steel. There was no such thing as a screw-in stud back then. We used to have leather studs which had to be hammered into the soles. They had three nails in each which, when the boots got old, would come through the sole and into the bottom of your foot. The two best things that came in handy in those days were the metal last my dad kept in the garden shed and inner soles.

With Southampton Schoolboys, we played for the English Schools Trophy. I always wanted to play in that tournament because I used to regularly look through the Charles Buchan football annuals and they always mentioned the competition. In 1960, we got to the sixth round. We had beaten the Isle of Wight, Slough Town, North Devon and Acton. We had scored 16 goals and conceded one. We were on a roll and next we had to play against West Ham. John Charles played for them, not *the* John Charles, but the black player who went on to play for West Ham professionally. They also had

John Sissons on the wing. They were a bit special and we got slaughtered 5–0 on a very heavy pitch. The teams were like chalk and cheese and I really learnt a lesson that day. We played for fun, they played to win – that was the difference. They were all affiliated to West Ham and they had a different approach to the game, a very professional attitude. It was like the difference between a Premiership club and a Second Division club. Compared to them we were a soft touch. That's when we found out we weren't as good as we thought we were.

At 16, I was selected for the Southampton youth team and at the same time I left grammar school. It was a massive decision. I had passed five O-levels in geography, maths, geometrical drawing, handicraft and German. I could have stayed on at school but I knew I was good enough to play professional football. In fact I had a meeting with the headmaster of the school about this very subject. His name was Charles Challacombe. I told him my plans and he said to me, "Only leave this school if you can be a Terry Paine." At that time Terry was the Southampton winger and knocking on the doors of the England team. He said, "If you feel you can reach that level I won't stand in your way. But all I am telling you is that you will have a very good education here. You can stay on and get A-Levels in maths, German or geography and then go on to university." But I knew that having rubbed shoulders with boys who were going to sign professional terms, I could match them. After all, I had started off very well in the youth team. After I left the school I scored four against Millwall in an away game that we won 6–1. This resulted in my first write-up in the local paper, which appeared alongside a picture of me:

> *"Martin Chivers, a former Taunton's schoolboy, scored four of the six goals including a second-half hat-trick and with a little more determination would have had more."*
>
> ***Southampton Evening Echo*, 31st October 1961**

I was on my way in the big wide world.

CHAPTER TWO

TED BATES AND THOSE RED-AND-WHITE STRIPES

You have to have a break in life. Mine came in the early autumn of 1961. One day the old man came back from the docks with the *Southampton Evening Echo*. He put it in front of me and showed me an advert. "Son," he said, "they're asking if anybody wants to write in for a trial with Southampton." Can you imagine that now, a club of that stature advertising for players? Incredible. Anyway, of course I said, "I'll do it."

All my friends in the Southampton youth team were apprentice footballers with Southampton FC and I couldn't understand why the club hadn't taken me on. I had played as well as anybody and had regularly scored goals. So around the time the advert came out, I was a bit down. That's when it all began to change. I wrote in for a trial in August 1961. I got it, played a game, scored four goals in the first half and at half time they had the forms ready for me.

I was signed up, not by the club directly, but by CPC Sports, the nursery team for Southampton FC. The organisation was run by a Charles Henwood, Managing Director of CPC, a local engineering firm that made big metal hoppers for grain. Henwood was so in love with Southampton Football Club he ran the nursery teams for them. At Southampton, if you were a promising player and the club wanted you, you would play for CPC Sports until you were good enough to sign professional forms. I went to work for them as a clerk. The job involved dealing with figures so it was an obvious choice for me. It wasn't serious. I was really a tea boy, doing a few odd jobs and a bit of clerical work, biding my time until I had the chance to sign professional forms. I earned three pounds seven and six a week.

Some of the boys playing with me were apprentices, so they were earning a bit more money and getting their digs paid. One of those boys eventually came to live with me and my family. He came down from Corby near Northampton. He had been living up the road with the other boys in Shirley but we got on so well together he became like a brother to me. His name was Norman Dean and I still see him to this day. He was inside forward and I was centre forward. Most of the guys who played in that team socialised together. There was a group of us – me, Norman, Bobby Wilkinson from Colchester,

Dennis Hollywood and Jimmy Burton from London – who used to go out together in Southampton. We'd go to coffee bars mainly. We also joined a youth club who we played cricket for in the summer. Norman came to the youth club and that's where the relationship built up. He came to my house a couple of times and we got on very well. My mother liked him, my brother had moved out and there was a spare bed going so Norman moved in. Naturally.

At the time I was training two evenings a week with Southampton. They had a very small ball court underneath the main stand that was about six yards wide by 30 yards long and we used to go there and basically kick shit out of each other. That was where I first learnt how to jump tackles. We also trained in the car park, which gave us a bit more room to practise shooting. It was a truly professional set-up! I was getting close to my dream and then it happened. I had played many games for the Southampton A team and I had scored numerous goals. I'd also played a couple of games in the reserves even though I wasn't technically signed for them. I had played with people knocking on the door of the first team and I had held my own. I even had an approach from a guy called Arthur Cox, a scout for Portsmouth, who came up to me as I was watching a game and asked me if I would be interested in signing for his club. There wasn't anything illegal about it, I was on the books at CPC and I was an amateur. I said, "With respect, if I am going to do anything, Southampton is going to be my first choice." At the same time, Southampton had started the season poorly – they had got one point from their first five games – and I began to hope that Ted Bates would soon be taking notice of me.

One Tuesday evening at training, Bates called me into his office. This was the first time I had ever been in there. I only ever went into it once more in my career. He looked up at me and he said, "Martin, I would like to come round and see your parents this Thursday evening if that is possible." As soon as he said that I was thinking something really interesting was coming my way. Then again there was a possibility he might have something different in mind. Perhaps Arthur Cox had approached him and he was willing to let me go to Portsmouth. I just didn't know. I knew Southampton would be silly to let me go, especially to their bitterest rivals.

Ted made an appointment to come round to my house at six o'clock. It had to be in the evening because my dad worked on the docks until five. Mum and Dad were so excited. I remember we had to tidy up everything. There was a front room in our house that we only used at Christmas and on very special occasions and we prepared that. We had a special china tea set that we had got from Germany, beautiful cups and saucers, and they came out too. I think my mother and father were more nervous than me. They knew of Ted Bates. He was a Southampton legend, a hero. He had played for

Southampton, coached Southampton and now managed Southampton. Ted Bates *was* Southampton.

Ted arrived on the dot of six and parked his enormous shiny car outside the house. He got out wearing a dark suit and tie. He was always dressed immaculately. When you saw him at the football club he always had a tracksuit on but this was official business. He didn't have much hair. He had been in football for so many years he had worn most of it away. He came in, sat down, and made a bit of pleasant conversation. Finally he said to my parents, '"Your young lad is doing very well; he has knuckled down. We are very pleased with the way he has developed. He has really come on in leaps and bounds. I really think that Martin can make a go at becoming a professional footballer and I have come round today to ask whether you would allow him to sign on as a professional at Southampton. I am sure he would like to, because I know the lad."

He was basically asking my parents their permission for me to sign to his football club in the way someone asks a father for their daughter's hand in marriage. He was very correct. My mother looked up and said, "Let's face it Mr Bates, the boy has always wanted to be a professional footballer. There is no way we are going to stand in his way. He left Taunton's when he had a great opportunity to carry on to university. He has wanted to be a footballer all his life and we are certainly not going to stop him now." Ted then turned to me and said, "What about you son? I suppose you want to sign?"

"Yes please," I gasped. He got the forms out of the envelope and I signed. It was a three-year contract and my wages were three times as much as I was getting at CPC. Ted put me on £9 a week basic and a £20 signing-on fee. If I played in the first team I got £25 a week. Then he dropped his bombshell. "Now this is going to be a surprise but you know that my first team are not doing very well, so I would like you to play on Saturday against Charlton." This was on a Thursday night. I had just signed professional forms and he wanted to put me in the first team straight away. I couldn't believe it. My parents were ecstatic. My dad was on top of the world. Although he didn't show a lot of excitement I could tell how thrilled he was. My mother was cock-a-hoop as well.

On Friday morning I travelled to The Dell, where I was introduced to the players. Then we had a team talk. I remember Ted sat us down on the ground towards the Milton Road end with all the players looking very serious and waiting to hear what he was going to say. He explained that there would be changes on Saturday. He announced that I was playing instead of Derek Reeves. That was the big shock to everyone in the team, especially Derek Reeves. He was a hero, he had scored something like 47 goals just a couple of seasons before but he had not been playing well recently. Even so, to bring in a boy who had just signed professional forms to replace him? I must have been making some impression for Ted Bates to take such a gamble.

After the team talk we did some very light training and I then had my first photographs taken as a professional footballer. They took shots of me wearing that famous red-and-white-striped shirt, stooped down by the goalpost, and then others of me shooting the ball into the net. It was one of the latter which made the front page of that Friday evening's *Southampton Evening Echo*.

I remember waking up on the morning of 8th September 1962 full of nervous excitement. I slept in to kill some time and came downstairs not knowing what to eat. The team never used to meet before a game, so they left you to your own devices. I just had to turn up at the ground at half past one. I had something very light to eat, cleaned my boots and pottered around the house. I remember the clock taking ages to move. Finally, it was time. We got in the car and my mother and father drove me to the ground. We parked in the car park – the same car park we trained on – and I realised there was literally nowhere for them to go while they waited for kick-off. The Dell was in the middle of a residential area with no shops or cafés around. There was one corner sweet shop and that was it. There was no player's lounge for them to sit in, so they had to stay put.

There were quite a few cars in there already – directors and whatever – so they couldn't drive off, otherwise they would have lost their spot. I remember that I went in, got changed and then I came out with the two complimentary tickets for them. I bumped into people we knew coming into the ground – I had no idea they went to games. They were from the Millbrook area where I lived – shop owners, plumbers – and there I was standing in my kit as they walked past. You might ask why I had got changed so early but throughout my career I have always needed an hour and a half to get ready. I am very fussy because I have to be comfortable in my boots; it is crucial to me. There is nothing worse than putting them on, finding you have tied the laces too tightly and you are onto the pitch and it's too late to sort them out. If you tie them well before the game, they settle in.

All the team had arrived by now and we were in the dressing room, waiting. I remember all the players in the team that day – Ron Reynolds, Ron Patrick, Tony Knapp, Cliff Huxford, Tommy Traynor, Ken Wimshurst, David Chadwick, George O'Brien, Terry Paine – of course – and John Sydenham. All of them were good to me. Some of them looked up and said, "Come on Chiv, this is your chance. You can do it." I remember Ted Bates talked to every player and kept saying to me, "Martin, just go out there and play your normal game and keep looking to get behind their full backs," Bates had put me up front with George O'Brien. I felt I wasn't big enough to play there just by myself because of the tackles in those days. I was only 11 stone and at that point in my career, I preferred to drop off a little and run at people.

The dressing rooms were in one corner of the stadium and you had to go down 20 steps to get onto the pitch. I always said that those 20 steps were the 20 steps of doom, even if it had always been my ambition to go down them and come out onto the pitch wearing that red-and-white shirt of the first team. Now I was about to do exactly that.

I was very nervous but I had played at the Dell before with the youth team, so I knew what the pitch was like. What I didn't know was what it was like to step onto the pitch in front of 30,000 people. The noise was overwhelming but I also made a strange discovery about playing professional football and it remained the same throughout my whole career. Before a game, you wind yourself up in the dressing room. You hear the faint murmur of the crowd and you concentrate. Then you go out and the atmosphere hits you. It is the most incredible adrenalin rush. But once the whistle goes you do not hear the crowd. You hear the din, but not the individuals shouting.

That afternoon, I remember the Salvation Army Band were on the pitch entertaining the crowd as we walked out. They played before every home game. As we came onto the pitch they began playing *When the Saints Go Marching In*.

At either end of the pitch, behind the goals, there were walls at least four feet high and very close to the goal line. Many footballers I've spoken to since say they always felt intimidated playing at the Dell. Another feature of the ground was that at half time, two men would walk round the pitch holding a blanket and fans would throw any spare coins into it. Then, at the end of the season, the fan club would count all this money and give it to the club along with other donations. There used to be sums of £1,000 or more raised, a huge amount in those days. There was also a cheerleader, a fella who was very similar to the guy who used to cheerlead at the England games. He had a rattle and he would go round the ground and gee the crowd up. I remember noticing that a boy that I used to play with in my primary schooldays was out there with him. His name was Graham Shaw and I used to envy him like hell. Now here I was playing for the first team. Incredible.

The game started and I just ran my socks off. I was marked very closely by Marvin Hinton but I think I did well enough to prove to them that I was a potential player. I did lay on a couple of chances for George O'Brien and one cross for Terry Paine, who unluckily saw his header crash against the crossbar. We won 1–0 and I provided the pass to O'Brien to score. It was a real physical game and, remember, I was a 17-year-old who hadn't fully matured. In those early days I was always aware of people coming in from behind. One nasty tackle in those days could put you in hospital and out of the game for weeks.

Anyway, after the game in the dressing room all the players had smiles on their faces. Terry Paine and Tony Knapp both came up to me and said, "Well played," which was satisfying considering I hadn't scored my usual goal. After I had showered and changed, I came out into the car park and my mother and father were standing there, looking so proud. It really made me happy to see their faces. Dad was not the greatest talker. He would tell me I had a fair game and he would praise me but then he would also tell me what I didn't do and where I had gone wrong. He was my biggest critic. I learnt not to get upset. Once I had started playing regularly I knew he used to go down to the docks proud as punch, especially when I'd scored on a Saturday. He never told me but I knew because his work-mates told me.

> *"Young Chivers was not overawed by the occasion and up front there was a great improvement. He did not get much change out of Marvin Hinton but his passing was accurate and he moved well. He had a match of which he could be well pleased. He did not score but he came very close, providing the pass for the goal. I thought Chivers showed he has a head for the game by the way he moved into good positions and by the thoughtful way he gave passes. Now that he is a full-time pro he can make big strides forward, the forward line worked much better than in previous games."*
> ***Southampton Evening Echo*, 12th September 1962**

After the game I felt a bit of exhilaration but, to be honest, I was pissed off I hadn't scored. That's just the way I was. I had to wait for the next game which was Chelsea away on the Monday evening. I didn't even get time to train with the team. We had Sunday off and then on the Monday we met to take the train up to London Waterloo, where we got a coach to Stamford Bridge. Chelsea were a very professional outfit. Peter Bonetti was in goal, they also had Eddie McCreadie, Bobby Tambling and Terry Venables.

I mentioned before that when I played against West Ham Schoolboys we got stuffed 5–0. They were totally professional compared to us: we played football for enjoyment but they played it to win. It was exactly the same against Chelsea: there was a big gap in class. Their football was slick and professional. We weren't as fit as they were and they ran us ragged. They won 2–0. They had something like 30 shots at goal and we had eight. Ouch.

> *"Young Martin Chivers, who made a promising debut on Saturday, found himself out of his depth against a strong Chelsea side. I do not think he is yet ready for Second Division football."*
> ***Southampton Evening Echo*, 13th September 1962**

After the Chelsea game the manager, much like the man in the newspaper, thought I was slightly out of my depth. He was right. I wasn't physical enough and

I needed building up. I was disappointed and I knew I wasn't yet ready, but then I thought to myself, "How's your luck?" In my second game, two days after my debut, I played against Chelsea away, one of the best teams in the league. They went close to winning the league that year, but still finished second and were promoted. In the meantime, Southampton bought another striker called George Kirby and he was an out and out animal. He was the total opposite to me – he went for people and intimidated opponents. George never had the touch or skill that I had but he didn't half frighten a few people. I saw goalkeepers conceding goals because they were more worried about where George Kirby was than concentrating on the ball.

So Bates put me back in the reserves and that's where I continued my apprenticeship. It was an enjoyable time playing up front alongside my mate Norman, with both of us scoring goals alongside many of my other friends from the youth team. I was getting better at shielding the ball and my dribbling was improving. I had a lot of skill for a big man. I had a good touch, therefore I was always on my toes – to the point where people used to think I was a bit of a fairy. If a defender came in for a 50-50 I wouldn't try and win the ball with a hard tackle: I'd try and get to the ball a split second before the defender, nick it away from him and then carry on. I very rarely went to ground. Possession of the ball was everything. I loved running with it and, like when I was running at school, because of my style my pace was deceptive. Players didn't think that I could get away from them but I had a long stride and a delicate touch.

In the reserves I got a lot of chances, some of which I would miss, but Ted Bates always said to me, "You've got to miss 'em to score 'em." So that became my attitude. I did make some memorable cock-ups, though. Playing Brentford away, I surged through their defence and then passed the ball square to my partner, thinking he would score easily. In fact, I had passed the ball to a Brentford defender. I had forgotten they were playing in red-and-white stripes and we were playing in our away kit.

At the same time as I was progressing in the reserves the first team went on a good FA Cup run. They got through to the quarter-finals and played Nottingham Forest at home. It was an incredible game. Southampton were 3–0 down at half time and then George Kirby started going for the goalkeeper and frightened the life out of him. In those days you could get away with it. Kirby terrorised him and we came back and drew 3–3, with their keeper practically throwing one into his own net for the equaliser.

The replay was held at White Hart Lane. I travelled with the team and I sat in the stands. It was the first time I had visited the ground which would dominate so much of my life. I was so envious of our players. I thought I was good enough to be in the team, so it was difficult to sit by and observe. I couldn't wait to get on a field and play in that sort of arena. To play at White Hart Lane, under those lights and in that atmosphere, was any player's dream. Southampton played out of their skin and we won 5–0. Ken Wimshurst was the star man. But then we were drawn against Manchester United in the semi-final and lost 1–0, Denis Law scoring.

At the beginning of 1963 there was a cold snap, so cold they called it the Great Freeze. We had a home game on Boxing Day and the snow started just after kick-off. By half time they were brushing the snow off the lines to make them visible. We just managed to finish the game and I don't know how we got home. It didn't stop snowing for 48 hours. That was only the start of it. We had eight weeks off from professional football. England was like the Arctic, with the snow about three feet high. When we could get out for training, we had to go up to the common, which was not far away from The Dell. We would try and find some footwear that would stop us slipping and sliding, but we still trained in those icy conditions. The only alternative was to play small-sided games in the ball court. When the snow finally melted, I continued playing very well for the reserves, scoring regularly or setting them up.

"Chivers led his line with such skill and gave Bill Dodgin such a harrowing time that he probably delayed the exile from centre half's return to the Fulham first team. Sound

in the air, he controlled the ball beautifully. Chivers might have had half-a-dozen goals."
***Southampton Evening Echo*, March 1963**

In April I got selected for the first team again for a match against Newcastle away. I got the chance because George Kirby was injured. I thought, "Newcastle away – how lucky can you be? Chelsea away then you get Newcastle away." I don't think I played that badly against a strong Newcastle team, and I did score our only goal in a 4–1 defeat. It was a header from about seven yards out and it was my first goal for the Southampton first team. It didn't do me any good, though. The next week, I went back to the reserves.

CHAPTER THREE

WHEN THE SAINTS GO MARCHING IN

I had a feeling the 1963/64 season was going to be my year. I was in a hurry to become a first-team regular but I started the campaign where I'd finished the previous one, in the reserves. But my moment wasn't far off. In fact, it came in October when the reserves played Southend United. We won 6–1, I got two goals and to cap it all, Ted Bates was present because the first-team game had been postponed. What a stroke of luck. I had a fair idea something might happen when I read his quote in the paper the next day.

> *"Several of the young players are developing well and knocking at the door of the first team, Chivers, indeed, did well in the forward role."*
> ***Southampton Evening Echo*, 7th October 1963**

I got a hat-trick in my next game against Aldershot and the following week, I replaced George O'Brien in the first team to play Swindon.

At that point in the season Swindon had not lost a home game and had scored 21 goals on their own turf. Nearly every chance I'd got in the first team had been away. I'd only played once at home, now there was Swindon who had this fantastic record. Mike Summerbee and Ernie Hunt were in the Swindon side and it was a heavy, muddy pitch. They went 1–0 up. I provided the pass for Terry Paine to score the equaliser. Then I got a chance midway through the second half, turning and hitting a good shot from the penalty spot with my right foot which flew in the back of the net. It was a very important goal, not just in the context of the game, but for my own career too.

From then on I became an ever-present in that team.

> *"Chivers crowns fine display with winning goal at Swindon. Outstanding performances given by two players brought into the side, Chivers and Ken Wimhurst."*
> ***Southampton Evening Echo*, 15th October 1963**

The Southampton first team that I was now part of had some great players. Terry Paine ran the whole show. He was a major character who had played about 800 games for Southampton, which is still a record. He was from Winchester and was an England international who played in the 1966 World Cup. He was a fantastic passer of the ball, quick and nippy with great vision. He couldn't run as fast as I could over a sustained period, but he worked tirelessly up and down the right side. He also got stuck in. He used to antagonise his opposition full back and even to this day I get people coming up to me and saying, "You played with Painey didn't you? The dirty little bastard." He always used to hang his foot out and catch opponents. Ted Bates used to say to me, "Watch the little fella, you'll learn a lot off him. If there's a train coming into the station, Terry will be the first one to see it coming in, he is so aware."

We struck up a great partnership. If I could find space to run into, Terry would always find me with a good pass. On the other side we had a good left-footed winger, John Sydenham, who was like an express train. We used to say, "Open the gates" because when he started running, he was just like a greyhound. So we had pace on one side and guile on the other.

Tony Knapp was captain at this time and he had a bad stutter. In fact it was so bad that when he had to decide which end to play at when he went up for the toss, the referees would tell him, "Point at the head or tail before the coin is spun, Knappy, otherwise you will never say it before it hits the ground and we'll be here all day trying to work out which end you want." We also pleaded with him not to ask any questions in the team talks because we didn't want to be in there all day.

After I came into the team, we won five games on the trot. Then Ted Bates, in his wisdom, decided he was going to take us to the Butlin's Ocean Hotel in Brighton over New Year before we played against Manchester United in the third round of the FA Cup. It was my thirteenth game and I was only a young lad of 18. On the way down on the coach we asked Knappy what the pools results were. We were all in a syndicate putting in a couple of quid each which was a lot of money in those days and if you picked out ten results from the Pools you could win at 60–1. We were all looking back at Knappy checking the results and he's saying, "Yes, got that one, got that one, Chelsea, yes," so therefore we only needed one more as we've got nine out of ten. Everyone is getting really excited: "What's the last one, Knappy?"

"F-f-f-f, F-f-f . . ."

"Fulham?" we all shouted.

"No, no, not them."

"F-f-f-f . . ."

"Forest?"

"No, not them."

"F-f-f . . ."

"Falkirk?"

"No."

"Who the hell is it then?"

"It's f-f-f-f-fucking Manchester United. The bastards drew!"

We never did win.

We arrived on the 29th to do some training on the hills in the area. On the 31st, New Year's Eve, we were in the bar and all these girls who worked for Butlins – the Redcoats – were in there too. Of course the players were straight into them. I didn't drink much in those days, especially when there was a big game coming up, but the rest of the team liked a drink. No one said anything about excessive drinking. It was just the culture in those days. It was about half past eleven and everything's starting to boil up when Ted Bates looked up at me and said, "About time you went to bed, isn't it son?" I said, "Okay boss," and he gave me a stick of chewing gum. "Chew on that," he said. That was his answer to everything. Rather than have me go and chase women or think about them all night, he gave me a piece of gum to chew on.

I went to my room and was trying to get to sleep but it was impossible with so much noise going on down the corridor. At one point, I poked my head out of my room and there were all these Redcoats ducking and diving in and out of rooms. There was an almighty ruckus. Jimmy Gallagher, the physio, appeared and he started turfing all these women out of the players' rooms. There was a lot of wrist-slapping and so on. We went out training the next morning and we acted professionally afterwards, but what do you expect if you take players to Butlins over New Year?

Before every game Ted Bates was very thorough. He'd go round and talk to every player, talk about tactics, how we were going to do it. He would tell me to try and be a bit more mobile, use the space behind full backs, get on the end of things but keep on the move. That was what he always used to say to me: "Keep on the move." I tended to be a bit static up front because I was frightened to go into other people's positions. But he got me to move right across the front line because that's what I needed to do: I needed to get away from defenders.

In those days, defenders would mark me man for man. But if I could lose my man I would always get in on goal. Playing against Manchester United on a muddy pitch at the Dell was my biggest challenge yet. Their team included great names like Charlton, Crerand, Foulkes, Cantwell and a very young George Best. Maurice Setters was marking me, and he took no prisoners. The game had barely started when suddenly we went one up, Terry Paine scoring with a header. Then, just before half time, I got the ball on the edge of the box, twisted in and out of a couple of players and let fly with my left boot. The ball flew into the top corner of the net.

The whistle blew for half time and all we were thinking was, "Christ, all we've got to do is stop them now." Unfortunately, we ran out of steam. I think Butlins caught up with us a little. United had a very good team and showed their class in the second half, where they ran out 3–2 winners. We really should have kept having a go at them but at least we were now beginning to play some decent football. A good team was starting to come together.

A few games later, I got sent off for the only time

in my career. We were playing Crystal Palace and came up on the train before boarding the coach for the trip to south-east London. But the driver went completely the wrong way. He somehow drove north over the river and suddenly we were caught in the thick of rush-hour traffic. It was five o'clock and we had a half seven kick-off on the south side of the Thames. We got the skip with all the kit out and started stripping off on the coach – bare arses in the windows. We arrived at Crystal Palace two minutes late and got fined.

We went to the dressing rooms for a quick pee and then straight out on the pitch. For the first 20 minutes I was having the shit kicked out of me by Alan Stevenson, their centre half. After a while I thought, "Hold on a minute, this is enough" and I retaliated. I kicked him from behind – hardly subtle I know, but nothing compared to what he was doing to me. Unfortunately, the whole world and its aunt saw the kick. The linesman signalled to the referee and that was it. I was off. I did learn my lesson though. I never got sent off again in my whole career.

We respected referees in those days. Very often we'd meet them on end-of-season tours and realise that they were fallible like everyone else. Plus there wasn't so much pressure on the games in those days and there were no cameras to prove them wrong. What the referee said was the end of it all.

Although we were playing good football there were games that went horribly wrong. I remember playing

Swansea away and losing 6–0. It was a very wet evening and in those days Vetch Field – Swansea's ground – was a quagmire. They had a big centre half called Herbie Williams and if they got a corner, I was supposed to come back and mark him. The first time that happened, Knappy looked up and said, "I'll take him." I think Herbie scored four goals that night. Thank God I didn't mark him because I would have been slated.

The season ended well. Southampton finished fifth in the league and I scored 21 league goals in 28 games. It was a wonderful time. I was a local boy and I had my picture in the paper every week. I was used to having my picture in there as a schoolboy but to be in there as a professional footballer, that was my dream. At Southampton the fans just accepted people: you were just a fella doing a football job and they hardly ever asked for autographs. If I went into town I wouldn't get the same adoration that I later got at Tottenham. However, in the 1960s, autographs didn't mean anything. You'd sign a photograph and never thought one day it might be worth something.

While all this was going on, I met a pretty girl called Carol Evans at a youth club. She came from the other side of Southampton. We started chatting, made a date and everything developed from there. It was a very simple courtship. Carol and I would go to the cinema every now and again but it was more of an outdoor life we led. With friends, we'd go and see the boats or we'd go down the recreation ground –

although she never played in goal like Pauline. We played golf in the afternoons or went ten-pin bowling. I even won a trophy at ten-pin bowling, scoring about nine strikes in a row and making a score of 262 – the maximum is 300. Other times we might go round someone's house and play records and dance. Music was very important to us in those days. I was a fan of Elvis, Buddy Holly and Eddie Cochran. I remember standing for ages in front of a mirror trying to blow-dry my hair so it looked like Billy Fury's – big quiff in the front and a DA at the back.

Back then, people expected you to be married by 21 or else there was something wrong with you. So Carol and I went out together for two years and then we got married. That's just what people did in those days. Looking back, if I am honest, I guess I was a bit naive and even though my parents liked Carol, they felt it was too early to get serious.

I bought a house in nearby Bassett which cost me £3,800. I had been careful with my money and had saved a lot of my wages – which were £25 a week – which is how I got to buy a house so early on in life. I was doing something most people couldn't afford. The average wage then must have been about £3 a week and getting a deposit together for most was very hard. I remember my teammates coming round to help me paint the house because I couldn't go up a ladder – still can't, well not a long way up anyway. I don't mind going up in a cable car or in an aeroplane, but a ladder is the end of the world. So it was a pretty daft idea when Norman and I started a house-painting business together. We had done such a good job on mine and my mum's house that we thought it a great plan. We had a good set of ladders going to waste and spare afternoons were the ideal time for us to do jobs on other people's houses. Norman always had to paint the top half of a wall or we would only accept bungalows. However, work hardly flowed our way. For some reason, I think people wanted professional painters and decorators and the idea was soon put aside.

The 1964/65 pre-season started for us in the second week of July. It was always the hardest part of the year, with all the stamina running, sprinting and weight training we had to do twice a day. We did not touch a ball for a week and when we did it was only in small-sided games. During training games one of Ted Bates's ploys (Bill Nick also did this later at Tottenham) was to switch the whole front line and make them play defence, and vice versa. So I would play centre half and the centre half would play centre forward. Playing in that position really gives you a good insight into a defender's mind. For example, it shows you how difficult it is for a centre half to mark a mobile centre forward. I learnt a lot from exercises like this.

The season started badly. In fact, we hit bottom spot quite early on. Then in September we went on a six-match winning sequence. In one of those games we beat Portsmouth at Fratton Park 3–0 and our fans invaded the pitch after the first goal, starting a fight with the Portsmouth supporters. In truth these derby games were nothing like the Arsenal-Tottenham battles. For one thing, Portsmouth weren't always in the same division as us so we only came up against them occasionally. The cities had so much in common. It was another port town not too far away and we were both teams who were striving to improve ourselves. I have to say that Southampton were the more progressive team. I can't ever remember losing against Portsmouth.

One thing I do recall from this period was that defenders were now looking out for me as I had earned a reputation. You have to understand that centre halves in those days may have been a little on the slow side but, my God, they did kick people. There were some animals at that time, out-and-out thugs. I can honestly say that half of them wouldn't get a game these days and if they did, they certainly wouldn't stay on the pitch. They went right through you to get the ball. I used to dread those first 15 minutes of a game on a muddy pitch. I'd think to myself, "I'm going to get clattered any minute now."

You knew damn well what their manager had said to them, "Let him know you're there," because you had heard those immortal words in your own dressing room from your own manager about their centre forward. You waited for it and sure enough he'd come right through you and take your legs away. You'd look up to the referee and say, "Christ ref, what's this?," and he'd say, "He got the ball," even if he had only got a little touch on it. When I look back at it, it was disgusting, not like today's football. I would love to have played in today's game for that one reason – you wouldn't have to play with fear as a distraction. Mind you, we had our own assassins. Cliff Huxford was our main boy. Knappy also got stuck in and Dennis Hollywood and Tommy Traynor were as tough as old boots. Those four were as tough as any players around then.

Occasionally you played against a real talent. I played against John Charles in a 2–2 draw against Cardiff in those early days. He was marking me and went up for a corner. I went with him and once again Tony Knapp said, "Don't worry, I'll take him." The next thing I know Charles has leapt up as high as the bar and headed the ball into the top corner. I have never seen a player who could leap like him. He was incredible and he scored both goals. I thought he was an unbelievable player, so much so that when I was asked at the Millennium to name my three most influential players, I named Bobby Moore, John Charles and Bobby Charlton. John Charles got my second vote; he was so strong yet he was also a gentleman. Yes, he tackled hard but you knew he wasn't going to try and do you. He was a true, solid, great footballer. He was probably slowing up when he played against us, but he could still cover the ground fast. No wonder he was a king in Juventus when he went over there. I don't think he had one weak point.

From very early on I had trouble with my ankles. On matchdays Jimmy Gallagher, the Southampton physio, would always strap them up. He was an old army boy, Jimmy, a lovely man with a great big handlebar moustache. He'd be there for anything you needed if you were injured. During the week he'd recommend you do hot and cold in the showers, dip whatever part of you was injured into a hot bath and then into a cold one. He never used ice. If you were really injured and he wanted to get you fit again he would start using these kaolin poultices. Kaolin is a substance you boil up in a pot; it's like wet cement. You take it out and spread it onto some gauze, then put another gauze onto that like a sandwich. It's bloody hot. He'd slap it on your ankle and say, "Is that all right?" Then he'd put more on and then he'd put a soft crépe bandage around it. He said the hotter you could bear it, the better. Kaolin poultices were the bane of my life. At Southampton I had strapping round both ankles in all the matches and later at Tottenham I had my ankles strapped every day, just as a precaution. I always used to like them strapped a little bit high in a match to protect my Achilles tendon if anyone came in from behind. Anyway, I'm not blaming my ankles but I started off slowly that season, not scoring goals as regularly as I had done before and everyone was talking about it.

Newcastle v Southampton
"Martin Chivers found the attentions of John McGrath very frustrating and he had opportunities for very few shots."
***Southampton Evening Echo*, 29th August 1964**

Southampton v Northampton
"Chivers, though trying hard, could not seem to make contact at the right moment."
***Southampton Evening Echo*, 5th September 1964**

Southampton v Preston North End
"Martin Chivers, who has not at the moment quite found his form of last season, was well marked by Singleton . . ."
***Southampton Evening Echo*, 16th September 1964**

Maybe my mind had been taken off football a bit by Carol. Football had been my entire life up until that point and perhaps now I was with Carol, I needed to do some readjusting. I was just itching to score again. Towards Christmas, the drought ended and I started to find the back of the net on a regular basis. I could score all kinds of goals – headers, tap-ins, one-on-ones – it didn't matter to me, as long as that ball ended up in the net. That was all I worried about.

In training, I'd continually practise one-on-ones with the keeper. The coach would give you the ball outside the penalty area, you would run forward with it and decide whether to shoot or go round the keeper and score. By that Christmas I was back on form and enjoying my game. Against Rotherham we hammered in six and I got a hat-trick, and we also beat Plymouth 5–0 with me getting two goals.

> Southampton v Plymouth
> *"Lately Martin Chivers has sometimes been finding the going hard but he is now in excellent form. He scored a great goal and had an important part in three other goals."*
> ***Southampton Evening Echo*, 26th December 1964**

We finished fourth in the end and perhaps should have done better. Jimmy Melia was now in the squad. When he came to Southampton I would guess that his age would have been 33 or 34 but he always looked older because he was a bit short in the hair department. He was the sort of player who could get other people to play. Jimmy was a real asset. While he wasn't dynamic, he had endurance and he talked to players off the field. Ted Bates might have brought him in for his football experience because he felt he could get younger players to play better and to bring that experience that we seemed to lack the season before. It proved to be successful but unfortunately Ken Wimshurst eventually moved on and we lost a very good player.

The following season, the 1965/66 campaign, we made a great start. We won five, drew one and lost one of our first seven games. Against Bury at the Dell we won 6–2. George O'Brien got four and I set up a couple for him but he rarely did the same for me. The truth was George and I never got on as he always saw me as a threat. The next week I got the only goal against Coventry. I was playing against their captain, George Curtis, who was a mountain of a man and looked like a marine – crew-cut hair, thighs that would crack a walnut – a Coventry player through and through. You just had to look at some of those centre halves and they would frighten the life out of you. Yeats from Liverpool, Bobby Moncur at Newcastle, Charlie Hurley at Sunderland – they were the big ones. Duncan Forbes was Norwich's strong centre half but I always did well there. It's a friendly ground and I remember the game against them that season, playing well and scoring.

> Norwich v Southampton
> *"They produced a brand of fast, clever football that was good as anything I have seen from them. Chivers scored one magnificent goal with a great run before the second half was a minute old and he supplied all the passes for the three other goals."*
> ***Southampton Evening Echo*, 11th September 1965**

Christmas came and, as usual, a local farmer gave us a turkey each. The directors also sent every player a card, although we rarely ever mixed with them. Before each home game George Reader, the chairman, would come in and wish us well but that was all we ever saw of the directors. We all called him 'Mr Chairman' but we knew he knew nothing about football. There was a strict hierarchy at the club. You'd go into Southampton FC: the dressing rooms were to the right and directors' room was to the left, and you never went to the left. All we knew was Ted Bates. He did everything. The normal training sessions he organised ran on average for about an hour and a half in the morning and then, in the afternoon, because we got a bit bored, we'd sometimes go back and do extra training. We would do some weights or some shooting in the players' car park where there was a cage that we used as a goal. Norman Dean and I would rather go to the recreation ground to practise shooting on grass. If we had lost a game, Ted would come in and give us some stick. Nobody would say a word until he came to each player and went through their game. After his criticism, some players would answer back. On occasions, the dressing room became quite heated to the point of stand-up arguments but disagreements never left that room, and you certainly wouldn't read all about it in the newspaper the next day. Ted loved those arguments because it proved his players' passion for the game.

We played Cardiff away over Christmas and the ground was frozen solid. The only problem for me was that Jimmy Gallagher hadn't packed my rubber-soled boots and I only had studs with me. Jimmy Scoular, the Cardiff manager, found out and led me to their boot room where I selected a brand new pair of boots. With them I promptly scored a hat-trick in the 5–3 win. After the game I went to give him back his boots. "Don't worry, son. You can keep them but that's the last fucking time I'm going to do a favour for a player."

> Cardiff v Southampton
> *"The scheming Jimmy Melia plus the bewildering interchanging of Martin Chivers and Terry Paine proved too much for Cardiff."*
> ***Southampton Evening Echo*, 27th December 1965**

One of the reasons for my success – and the team's – was that I had built up an almost telepathic understanding with Terry Paine. We linked so well together. He had great vision and knew exactly where I wanted the ball and when. He was also deadly accurate with his passing. Our relationship worked both ways and I found him many times with some fantastic balls. I was flying this season, scoring goals all the time. I had found my feet. Norman Dean had eventually come into the first team and scored a hat-trick against Portsmouth and was in the side until the end of the season. Norman wasn't fast but he was a classy player; not as big as I was, but he certainly knew where the goal was.

Norman used to love scoring goals and we worked well together. I think it was because we knew each other so well. It's amazing what you can take on to the football field. If Norman went near post I would go far post and vice versa. We did it instinctively. In fact, Norman was probably a better header of the ball than I was at the far post. I was always better at the near post because of my speed in front of the defender. Once I got that half a yard on a defender, all I had to do was to concentrate and make good contact. More often than not, it hit the back of the net.

Charlton v Southampton
"Martin Chivers was the outstanding forward and his two goals were really fine ones. In the 16th minute he took a return pass from Terry Paine and crashed in a splendid goal. His second goal in the 81st minute was a header from a centre which full back Tommy Hare swung across."
***Southampton Evening Echo*, 4th December 1965**

By February of 1966 I had scored 30 goals in 29 league games. But then I twisted my back badly in training and I was unable to play again until mid-April. I couldn't push a door open, I had to learn against it and back into it, it was that chronic. The club medics tried everything. First came the rack. A belt was put round my waist which stretched me. It was bloody torture and it didn't work. I was sent to London with the physio, Jimmy Gallagher, because I was missing games and by now the club were panicking as there was a chance of promotion to the First division.

We had an appointment with a man called Dr

Cyriac who became very famous for treating back injuries. There was even a Cyriac's Method of trying to manipulate your back. Cyriac's surgery was in Tottenham Court Road where he instructed two nurses to take me to a room and strip me down. I was laid flat on a treatment table where these two good-looking nurses manipulated my back every 20 minutes for five hours. After that time, Cyriac came in and said, "Any difference?" but he knew there wasn't because as soon as I bent forward to touch my toes I was crippled with the pain again. Obviously there was something very, very wrong with my back. He laid me on my stomach and started the next procedure, giving me several painkilling injections around the base of my spine. Then, with a very large needle, he injected though the base of my spine to about the fourth vertebra. Jimmy Gallagher told me later that the needle was enormous. We returned immediately on the train. Thank God the pain began to ease after a week. To this day I don't know what was wrong. Meanwhile Mike Channon had taken my place in the team. He came from the sticks of Wiltshire with a broad country accent and was playing well. This was all I needed – struggling with this back injury which lasted to the end of the season and a young hotshot forward on my tail. I was really fearful for my place in the team.

I had gone nine games without scoring, yet I finished up with 30 goals that season. However, when I was not scoring goals I was not fun to be with.

During that time I was a miserable bastard at home and horrid to live with. I would not read the newspapers because my name wouldn't be mentioned. I would be irritable, off-hand with people. This meant that Carol and I wouldn't go out anywhere. I was in too bad a mood to see anyone because the last thing I wanted was for them to talk about football. The only thing I could do was keep playing and hope I could put things right.

In mid-April, I returned. In the league, Manchester City, Coventry City and Huddersfield Town were looking favourites for the two promotion places and Ted Bates came to me and said, "Martin, can you play?" Although I wasn't 100 per cent, I could run and straight away I told him, "Yes boss." No player who is asked to play by his manager would turn it down. I was no exception despite injury. The game was against Charlton at The Dell and it was a very tight game as they were fighting relegation. In the 89th minute it was 0–0. Then, I picked the ball up just outside our penalty box and I ran with it, passing the halfway line and heading for goal. I was lucky that nobody really challenged me because any body contact or twisting would have hurt my back so much it would have stopped my run. But because of my speed no one got near me so I thought, "Sod it, I'll keep going". I ran all the way down to the Archers Road end. To be honest, I didn't think anyone had kept up with me but I spotted Terry Paine running into the box and squared the ball to him. He scored with a shot he hit first time low into the net.

> Southampton v Charlton
> *"Chivers got possession from a David Webb pass deep inside the Saints half. Chivers, returned to the side after a back injury, had not been showing his best form, obviously feeling the effects of the injury, but when the chance came he rose to the occasion and raced away towards the Charlton goal. Speed and control were there for all to see as he ran fully 70 yards with Kinsey and Campbell following him. He called to Terry Paine to get into the middle. Paine raced to the centre of the goal ready to receive Chivers perfectly placed pass which he swept into the net. One would have thought that the goal actually ensured promotion by the wild reception it got from the crowd and when a few moments later the game ended, spectators invaded the pitch and carried some of the players in triumph to the dressing room."*
> ***Southampton Evening Echo*, 30th April 1965**

Even at this point we never really thought we could get promotion but Coventry started to falter. They were the favourites. They were there with Man City and both were leading the division. But they started losing and we got on a great run. For example, we did not expect to go down to Plymouth and win. Plymouth at home were a very useful side and hard to beat. But we beat them. I remember it well. It was a sunny day and it was a bumpy pitch. My back was still playing up so I wasn't scoring goals. I was all right to run in a straight line, but it was the manoeuvring, the changing of direction that I just couldn't manage. Still, at least I was big and I could win balls in the air. Of all the people to score on that day it was Jimmy Melia. If you look back at the records he was not renowned for scoring goals. At all. But he scored against Plymouth and that was probably the biggest shock. Not us winning but Jimmy Melia scoring a goal!

After that we had two games left, both away. Coming back on the train to Southampton we suddenly thought, "Hello, we have got a chance of winning promotion here" but it still depended on Coventry. We were now breathing down their neck. Then they slipped up again and we only had to get two points from our last two matches to guarantee promotion, a win or two draws, and even one point would probably be enough as we had a much better goal difference than Coventry.

We played Leyton Orient away and thousands of our fans came to the game. I think 6,000 of them descended on Brisbane Road. I don't know how many they squeezed into their ground that night – it was a fantastic, though very nervous, atmosphere. It was also a nervy game. They scored first but then Terry Paine equalised with a header. I can picture him now running in at the far post and heading that ball into the net.

Finally the whistle went and that was the cue for celebrations galore. Our fans swarmed onto the pitch and it took ages to get to the dressing room. In fact, most of us were actually carried off the pitch. In the dressing room the champagne was flowing. As long as we didn't lose by six or more goals in our final game against already promoted Manchester City we were up.

> Martin Chivers Post-match interview
> *"I thought we did well to come back from a goal down against a tight defence. It has been my ambition to play First Division football and now I can do this with the Saints. I don't think my back is 100 per cent yet but I get so disheartened when I am out of the team that I am not worth living with. Being Southampton-born I really want to do well for the supporters and goals are what they want from me. I have gone nine games now without a goal and it gets so frustrating but I must fight on and hope for a change of luck."*
> ***Southampton Evening Echo*, 9th May 1966**

Like all managers, Ted Bates was cautious in the run-up to our final game. It was the first time in the club's history that they were going to go into the first division so he had every reason to try and dampen our enthusiasm down a little bit. He took us to a hotel in Buxton up in the Pennines, just about the quietest place in the world. Maybe he was thinking about that Butlins incident all those years ago!

We arrived on a lovely day and went for a walk in the local park. We asked these old codgers if we could play a game of bowls and borrow their jacks. Footballers are always competitive and we played very seriously, with nowhere to go and nothing else to do. The next day we played Manchester City and drew the game 0–0.

Southampton had been promoted. It was a great feeling.

After the game Norman and myself went to the hotel's swimming pool downstairs and began being a bit silly, drinking champagne, splashing around and diving. At one point Norman dived in and stayed underwater for ages giving me the fright of my life as I thought he was a goner. That was our grand celebration.

A few days later Ted Bates came in and said, "We've been invited onto the *Queen Mary* by the captain." That afternoon we went down to the docks for tea on that magnificent boat. I had only ever seen the *Queen Mary* when she was in dry dock being overhauled so to visit her was like a dream come true. We are all dressed up with collars and ties and our Southampton blazers, going up the gangplank and who do I spot? My old man. He was working with a great, big hook in his hand. I had never been to see him at the place he had worked nearly all his life. And here he was, the first person I saw. I shouted "Hello" to him and he smiled back. Even so, I felt terrible. I just wished I could have taken him with me. It was some consolation knowing he was as proud as punch.

My father came to all our home games. He would go to work on Monday morning and everybody would say, "The boy did well then, Tom" and he loved it, although he was always critical of me if I didn't play well. If I had done OK he would say, "Well played," which was all he needed to say. He might add, "That second goal, you took that one well." But, like Ted Bates and later Bill Nick, he would always remind me of the one I missed. He would get a little quip in at the end like "Could have got four though . . ."

We were not granted a civic reception for getting promotion but we were given an audience with the mayor. In his parlour we had a glass of wine. The only player not there was Tony Knapp. He arrived an hour late. When he arrived we asked where the hell he had been. He said, "I'm cured. I've been to see this hypnotist and I'm talking to you now quite normally. I'm not stuttering, not catching my words, am I?" We said, "That's brilliant, Knappy, how did this happen?" His reply was, "If you look me straight in the eye, and you keep your eyes on me, I just don't stutter – I am cured." Of course at that we all looked away, some at the ceiling, some at the ground. "No, no, no, no, no," he cried, "don't look away 'c-c-c-cause I'll get it all wrong." We were a shameless bunch.

CHAPTER FOUR

GOALS, GOALS, GOALS

At the start of the 1966/67 season, the town was buzzing. Southampton had never played First Division football before and everybody was excited about welcoming the big teams and the big players to the Dell.

Ted Bates needed to start thinking about his squad for the demands of the First Division. So he bought Ron Davies from Norwich for £50,000 – the highest transfer fee the club had ever paid. It was great playing with Ron. He was so dynamic in the air and deft with his feet that I knew we were both going to score goals. He was one of the few players at the time who didn't run and take off with one foot, but jumped up from two feet. I liked to spring up from my left foot, which probably came from my high-jump days. I got on very well with him and if you have ever read his book, he says out of the two players he played with at Southampton, myself and Mick Channon, I was the better partner. Mick was a very good player, but as a partnership Ron Davies preferred playing with me because I laid things on for him. The sad thing about Ron's arrival was that Norman had to take a back seat. He left the club before I did and was soon on his way to Cardiff.

NORMAN DEAN ON MARTIN

I liked Martin. I liked his attitude, and we got on great. We never said anything against each other – unless he made a bad pass, of course.

We met at an evening training session either Tuesday or Thursday, in the car park with the lights on. We got to play together, got selected for the youth team and the A team and then the first team. We were both strikers, both goalscorers. There were a lot of good people in that team and we were good people as well. There is a lot of mickey-taking in football but we would back each other up. It was excellent.

In the morning when we went training we would get a lift from Cliff Huxford. He lived just around the corner and of course nine times out of ten Martin and I were late. We would be waiting anxiously at the bus stop and then Cliff would suddenly appear. We soon realised he was always late as well.

I was honoured to be asked if I wanted to live at

Martin's family house, which was great. His mum and dad were wonderful people and made it so much better than living in digs. I learnt to put salad cream on my chips at his house – that was one of Martin's tips. At night, we used to go out to youth clubs; I was there when he met Carol, his first wife.

He was a great striker of the ball; he could hit a ball so well. Once he got in his stride he was unbeatable. He reminded me of Bobby Charlton the way he could strike a ball. It was fantastic watching his career progress after he left Southampton. I was so proud of him, especially when he was chosen to play for England. That was great. I was so happy for him; he really deserved everything that came his way.

The top teams in that division were Tottenham, Chelsea, Liverpool, Manchester United, Manchester City and Newcastle and they were all very mobile. Chelsea gave us a taste of what to expect in one early game. McCreadie and Harris were solid defenders but they moved all over the pitch. Their defenders had as much skill as the strikers. Their movement upset us; we didn't have defenders who could cope with it. Usually in those days if a player had number 9 on his back you thought you knew what position he would be playing but Peter Osgood was everywhere. Ted Bates's reaction to all this was simple: we had to attain that same level of skill and that was the challenge for him. At the start of the season teams outnumbered us completely in midfield, so we had to start dropping back and working hard instead. We started off the season OK, losing just twice in ten games with Ron and I playing well. But in the next eight games we lost six times.

We went up to White Hart Lane to play Spurs in late November and it was the biggest crowd I'd ever played in front of – 60,000. I couldn't believe it. Of course, at that time, I never knew that the place would eventually become my second home. It was a magnificent, unique stadium and I always remember how imposing The Shelf was on that day. It was the best atmosphere I had ever experienced at that point in my career.

Dave Mackay or Phil Beal would have marked me that day and although we lost, we scared them with three goals. Not one of them had my name on it but although I did not meet Bill Nicholson that night, perhaps that was when I caught his eye. That said, I never dreamt of moving. I never thought, "Oh, I'd like to play for Tottenham every week." I was a Southampton boy and I wanted to do my best for them.

Although we were scoring goals we couldn't stop them going in, as the Tottenham match proved. For example, we let five in at home against Blackpool and now we slipped into the relegation zone. We were very attack-minded. It suited me in a way but at the same time we were always too top heavy, we weren't mean enough. The successful clubs didn't give too many goals away. Our first season in the top division was the hardest and even though we started off quite well we could never beat the big clubs. We were destined to be among the five or six teams at the bottom of that division fighting to ensure that we didn't go back down. All the big clubs were professional and strong – they were like tanks, they overpowered you. They were complete units and we were the ploughboys trying to pick results to save ourselves from relegation. Every club needed a dominating midfield player like Colin Bell, Emlyn Hughes or Alan Ball, someone who was dynamic, someone who was going to come forward and score goals as well as defend. We didn't have one player like that at Southampton.

At Everton I scored my 100th goal for the club but soon after I was dropped for the game against West Brom, with Mick Channon taking my place. I don't know why they were looking at the strikers as the problem because we were scoring goals all the time. Channon was banging them in for the reserves and maybe Bates felt he deserved a chance. In that game, Channon got injured in the second half and I came on and I scored. I was really happy to prove Bates wrong. In the next game we had to beat Nottingham Forest to stay up. I scored the first goal in 2–1 win and we finished the season 19th out of 22. We'd just done enough. It had been a disappointing season for the club but Ron Davies and myself had scored so many goals between us that a lot of people commented that we were one of the best partnerships they had ever seen in a red-and-white shirt. We scored 62 goals between us that season. He got 38 and I got 24. Not bad for a first season in the First Division.

That summer the club went to Kuala Lumpur on tour where all the American GIs from Vietnam were on leave. On arrival we had a big meeting in the hotel where our doctor told us, "Be very careful and don't be tempted by the ladies of the night because there's a very nasty disease going about over here and it can kill you." Thinking back it must have been a very early form of AIDS. We called it the Vietnam Strain and it frightened the life out of us. Needless to say we all stuck together going to restaurants and bars. All the players looked forward to the end of season tour because that's when you could let your hair down and enjoy yourself. It was when you really get to know your teammates. I learnt a lot of my golf on these tours and this was no exception. Norman Dean and I had started playing on the Municipal Club at Southampton and after 40 years I am not much better. Later Bill Nick would say he didn't like me playing too much golf. He said, "You're already laid back enough, I don't want you any more relaxed: go and play squash."

We played against Leicester in Kuala Lumpur and drew 3–3. Then in Ipoh, near the northern border, we played a very heated, volatile game against the local team. One of their defenders went down under a challenge from Terry Paine in the penalty area where Terry stupidly trod on his head. That was just the sort of thing Paine would do. The crowd went mad, absolutely ballistic and we had to come off the field as their fans were climbing over the fences to rush the field. We escaped back into the dressing room and the big debate was whether we would go back into the lions' den again. Ted Bates suggested we leave it for ten minutes to settle.

Listening to the baying crowd a couple of us jokingly said, "It's Painey's neck they want – send him out. He's the one that did it, let them sort it out with him and then we'll go and finish the game." Eventually Terry did indeed go out and bowed to the crowd in apology and shook the hands of their players.

It was the first time we had been to the Far East and the food was so different to what we ploughboys were used to. Kuala Lumpur was an intense, hot place and it was quite an experience. We were lucky to stay at the best hotels and we always had a roommate. I thought it wonderful to have someone to chat to and relax with in the room. Of course a snorer could put you off that idea but I always liked to talk about the forthcoming game or analyse the game that has just taken place.

We returned to England for several weeks off and then pre-season training started. Ted Bates tried to get us on grass as often as possible so we trained quite a bit at the BTC ground in Swathling. The team that season was essentially Martin, Webb, Hollywood, Fisher, Knapp, Walker, Paine, Davies, Melia, Sydenham and myself. Once again, Ron and I started off very well. It was an exciting partnership but our second season in the top division was to prove no different to the first, with too many goals flying in at the other end.

We won and lost games in equal measure. Our most memorable match that season was when we beat Chelsea 6–2 at Stamford Bridge. Ron scored four and I got two. In another game I made a mistake – I scored a goal against Liverpool. Bill Shankly must have had a little word with Ron Yeats, their centre half, at half time because he hammered me from behind about two minutes into the second half and I was carried off with a badly damaged ankle. That October I was named Player of the Month by the *Evening Standard* and awarded a cigarette lighter. Such a useful present for a professional footballer.

The Leicester game saw Peter Shilton, their goalie, scoring his first ever goal. He kicked the ball out of his hands; it landed inside our penalty area, skidded off the muddy surface and over Campbell Forsyth and into the net.

In September I was chosen for a Football League Eleven squad to play Belgium. It was bad timing because Carol was about to give birth to our first child, but I couldn't turn it down. This was the first time I had been selected for a senior international team.

Luckily, Carol gave birth to Andrea two days before I went away. Andrea was born on 25th September and the game was on the 27th. I was there for the birth, which took place at our home. We had a midwife come round very early that morning because Carol's contractions had started in the night. Carol was actually overdue but a friend of ours had told me to take her down a bumpy road in the car to help her along. Sure enough, I took her down a bumpy road and that evening the contractions started.

Throughout the night they got closer and closer so at six in the morning we called the midwife. She came round and started preparing everything. As she did I went for a walk up to the local pub to get some fresh air. I remember going into the pub's outside toilets for a pee and then I came back. The midwife could see I was very frustrated at not being able to do anything. She said, "Come up, you can help out." She gave me the gas and the air which I then administered to Carol so I was there when Andrea was born. I think having kids is a miracle. You count the toes and the fingers when they come out and you feel for your wife because she has gone through agonies but you can't help thinking that this is the miracle of life.

At the same time this was the first time I had been called up for a senior England team and Carol wouldn't deny me that even though she had just given birth. She knew it was something I had to do. I went to Belgium but I didn't play.

I did play for the same team, however, when I was selected again in November for a game against Ireland in Dublin and with that came the thrill of playing next to Jimmy Greaves. As far as I was concerned I was playing with the greatest goalscorer in the whole country. The pitch was a ploughed up field where they normally played rugby. It was really pleasing to score three goals, with Jimmy notching two. On returning to the hotel, I finished up in the bar in the company of Reg Drury, a reporter for the *News of the World*, and Jimmy Greaves.

It was Jimmy who looked up and said, "Would you ever consider moving to Tottenham?" I said, "Why do you ask?" and he replied, "I think they are looking for a player like you. Why don't you come and play up in London if you are interested." I told him that anybody would be excited by a move to Spurs. They have always been one of the top six clubs in the country. Reg quizzed me about my contract and asked whether the club would be willing to let me go.

People might be surprised that a journalist would act in this manner but Reg Drury was like an agent to me. That is because the payback to him was that if he wanted an article for the *News of the World* I would give him that article; I would give him an interview. You had to be careful because managers, Bill Nick especially, did not like you giving interviews to anybody. He wanted complete control of you and he didn't want anything controversial to go out. Yet whatever Reg wanted I gave to him. That was the unspoken deal between us. Looking back now, the conversation should not have taken place. It was, and still is, illegal to approach a player while he is under contract. Yet it planted an idea into my head.

By coincidence, our next game was against Tottenham at the Dell and although we lost 2–1, I scored our goal. Even more reason for them to like me. Not only was I thrilled at the thought of playing for Tottenham but I knew that doing so would boost my chances of playing for England.

The only way I could get a transfer was to put in a written transfer request. This meant that I would only receive five per cent of the transfer fee as opposed to the ten per cent you received if you moved without asking. I then went to see Ted Bates and talked to him. I said, "Look, you have got Mike Channon coming through. How about making some money and letting me go? You can't keep three strikers happy." He said, "No." I went back to him after a week or so and said, "Look Ted, this isn't going to work. You have got me, Ron and Channon to keep happy."

The most important thing for me at that time was to get the request accepted. It was obvious that Mike Channon was waiting in the wings and he was a perfect replacement for me. While I knew it would be a terrible wrench to leave my home town just as I had settled in my new house, and after having just started a family, I was quite willing to take up the challenge and move to London. Even though this move was uppermost in my mind, I still gave my best to Southampton. In the next two games against

Sheffield United, both at home and away, I scored in each game.

In the midst of all this, I received a phone call from Reg Drury saying to hold tight, that he understood Southampton were going to discuss letting me go at a board meeting that was due to take place that afternoon. He was right. The next day I went into Southampton on a shopping trip. It was there I saw on the *Southampton Evening Echo* billboards the headline, 'Record Transfer for Saints Star'. I went into training the next day and Ted Bates pulled me aside and informed me that I was now on the transfer list. Three clubs were interested in me – Stoke, Arsenal and Spurs. I dismissed Stoke because it was too far north. Arsenal never got in touch – thank God – as I don't think I could have been a success there. They built a team on the defence whereas Tottenham were a free-flowing, attacking team. Spurs, however, had it made very clear they were very keen to talk to me. They had gone out of the European Cup Winners' Cup to Olympique Lyonnais on the away-goals rule and I think this helped to convince them they needed someone like me up front. Ted Bates then told me that Bill Nicholson wanted to meet me. It would just be Bill and I at that first meeting and if that went well, Ted would then get involved.

I first met Bill Nicholson on Wednesday 10th January 1968 at Waterloo station. He had a florid, craggy face, and was smartly dressed and well groomed.

He was football mad and in that respect he reminded me of Ted Bates. All they ever talked about was football, knowing all the ins and outs of the game on and off the pitch. Most football managers were like that back then.

We met in a restaurant there. I did not make any demands as I felt I needed time and I was not going to say yes there and then. I don't think this went down very well with Mr Nicholson – he was expecting me to snap his hand off as most would have done. But I felt I had to speak with Carol and my family before making such a big decision. Certainly, I felt that Southampton were not going to be a force in the First Division as Tottenham were. If I wanted to play for England at full honours then they would be the perfect showcase for me.

The next day Ted Bates and I went and met Bill Nicholson in a hotel in Winchester. Ted drove me from The Dell and on the way there he said, "Martin, I am very reluctant to sell you but I understand your need to move on." I have to say I felt emotional towards Ted. He had been a great manager for me and helped my progress no end. We arrived at the hotel and settled in the lounge and waited. Bill arrived shortly afterwards. He and Ted knew each other and after formal greetings Ted turned to me and said, "Martin, as you know we are meeting here today to discuss your possible transfer and I will now hand you over to Bill." Bill then said, "After talking to many people I really think you can do us a world of good. I'm looking for a striker of your stature, your goalscoring ability and I think you will complement our team as the player you are." He said, "I've got Jimmy Greaves, Alan Gilzean, Dave Mackay, Pat Jennings and Cyril Knowles." He didn't need to sell the club to me but after he read out that list there was no doubt in my mind and I agreed to sign for the Spurs. The following day, which was a Friday, I went to White Hart Lane and signed the papers to make me a Tottenham player. I spent the next three days in Southampton and on Tuesday 16th January I travelled alone to King's Cross station and met up with my new teammates.

I was about to make my debut for Spurs and I had not even trained with them.

CHAPTER FIVE
THE LILYWHITES

People say it must have been tough going into that great Spurs team with all those international players. I always tell them it was the easiest thing I ever did. I loved it. I had been scoring goals at Southampton against all kinds of opposition so to go into a better team, surely I was going to score even more. We had Jimmy Greaves and Alan Gilzean (Gilly) up front, Cliffy Jones on the wing, Dave Mackay, Mike England, Joe Kinnear, Cyril Knowles, Alan Mullery, Terry Venables and Pat Jennings at the back. If you couldn't play in a team like that, who could you play for?

So there I was, five days after signing for Spurs, in the away dressing room at Sheffield Wednesday about to make my debut for the mighty Tottenham Hotspur. "We're not going training, are we?" I asked as a bundle was chucked at me across the dressing room by Cecil Poynton, the physio, kit man, sponge man, and general dogsbody at Spurs. I had arrived at Hillsborough expecting the same preparation as I had had before all previous matches with Southampton. That meant kit neatly folded and laid out especially for me in my place in the dressing room. "It's your kit," Poynton replied. I undid a crumpled up pair of shorts and an old pair of socks, one of which had a hole in. The shirt was like a map of Great Britain with all the creases. In fact, it was like a bit of clothing from a Dr Barnardo's home. "This can't be the match kit," I thought to myself.

I tried to put the shirt on but it was so tight and the sleeves were up by my elbows. As I was yanking at them to come down a bit, Pat Jennings was watching me and started to laugh. He shouted to Bill Nick, "Chiv's got a problem: he doesn't know whether he is wearing a short long-sleeved shirt or a long short-sleeved shirt." Bill's dour reply was angled directly at me. "Son, when you have proved to me that you're a good player you can have a decent shirt."

He had just bought me for a record £125,000 but felt I didn't deserve a decent set of kit. I learnt two big lessons in those few minutes. Whatever happened or was said or done in that dressing room was always passed through the manager. Secondly, I realised I could never take anything for granted with Bill Nick. Although our initial meetings had been cordial I soon understood that Bill was number one at the football club. It heralded the start of an enigmatic relationship, which neither of us would particularly enjoy or, indeed, understand.

In the first half I made a good run down the outside, squared it for Jimmy who side-footed it home. I felt great and a little relieved. It thrilled me to think that I had started to pay back a bit of my transfer fee so soon. Wednesday equalised, but ten minutes before the end I picked up the ball up on the halfway line and ran with it until about 25 yards out. It was then I smashed it with my right foot and saw it fly into the net above Ron Springett's head. I thought, "This is it, I've done it – another two thousand off that fee."

At the end of the game everyone was on an adrenalin high, jumping for joy, shouting what a result. I said, "We've just won a league game, what's so special?" – "You don't know, do you," the other players shouted back. "This is the first time we've beaten Sheffield Wednesday at Hillsborough in 31 years!"

In my first game, I'd already started breaking records, but although there was a smile on Bill's face I soon learnt how it worked. It was only there when you got results.

I lived for the rest of that season at the Alexandra National Hotel in Finsbury Park, where I put on half a stone in weight. This could have been the food or the weight training at Spurs. It was either fat or muscle and only time would tell which. It was there that the club sent a car for me to take to my next game, the derby against Arsenal at White Hart Lane. Normally the car would take half an hour to get to the club but it came an hour early, taking a shortcut down Lordship Lane where alarmingly we passed the red-and-white scarves of 15–20,000 Arsenal fans. Of course, all our fans were already there. We drove through those wonderful gates of that great stadium that I would get to know inside out.

In those days we were left very much to our own devices before a game. You were not told what to eat or what to avoid: you just sorted yourself out with a pre-match meal. You were trusted not to have a drink the night before, something that went without saying for me. In my entire career as a professional footballer I never went out the night before a game and I don't think many others did either. There might have been the odd idiot who wanted to take a chance and there were always rumours about players being seen out drinking but I stopped at that. My personal routine was to get into the dressing room about an hour-and-a-half before the game, relax, make sure my studs were right and have a look at the programme.

My ankles would then get strapped up which was the same routine for every Tottenham game the whole time I was there. I was a big fella and there was a hell of a lot of weight going down on those ankles. An inspection of my laces was next in the regime. I was anxious to avoid all disastrous eventualities where possible. So by about quarter-past-two, I was ready for the game.

Then I would take my boots off, just loosen them,

put them down by the peg and just walk about and chat with the other players. We never thought of doing a warm-up or going to the gym or anything like that before a game. Warm-ups back then meant a bit of an oil rub in the dressing room and a few stretches. Before most games, I'd be a bit nervous and go to the toilet a couple of times.

There, I would watch smoke coming out of the toilet next to me where Jimmy Greaves would be having his last cigarette. He was allowed to smoke in the toilet but not in the dressing room. Bill Nicholson would be going round the dressing room having quiet words with individual players and then he would address us all and give his final team talk. He would always say, "There are two games which are the most important of the season, today and Arsenal away." They were Bill Nick's big, big games. "Don't let the fans down." That was Bill's all-abiding message because the fans were the most important people to him. Then the buzzer would sound.

That day I couldn't believe how muddy the pitch was at White Hart Lane. The drainage had broken and gone to pot and their answer was to chuck loads of sand on top. But the atmosphere was unbelievable and the Spurs fans gave me the most tremendous reception as I came out of that famous tunnel. The place erupted. Unbelievable.

The game went by so quickly. I can remember being desperate to score. I was being marked by Ian Ure, who stuck to me all over the pitch to make sure I didn't. It was a good physical contest as he was six foot three. In the end Gilly scored the only goal of the game and in the dressing room afterwards everyone was on top of the world because we had beaten our arch-enemies.

I was absolutely knackered when Jimmy Greaves patted me on the leg and said "Well what do you think of that, big fella?" I gasped, "It was fantastic, unbelievable, but Jim, I can't play on that pitch, there's six inches of mud out there." I thought we were talking man to man, confidentially, but at the top of his voice Jim shouted across to Bill Nicholson, "Chiv's just told me he can't play on that pitch." I was so embarrassed I could have sunk into a hole but to Bill's credit his only reply was, "Well, I've got news for you son, you're playing on it every other week so you'd better get used to it." I got away lightly on that occasion.

Bill's remarks to me became more and more scathing as time went on. There were no secrets in the dressing room, although whatever happened in there never left it. In my time at Spurs there were lots of very heated arguments but they were always settled in that room and never made public. It was all down to respect for each other.

Next came another big game. Spurs had bought me to score the goals to defend the FA Cup they had won the year before. We now faced Manchester United. What's more we were travelling there not by train but by plane. Flying to a game in England was a completely new experience to me. I'd like to say it was a thrill but I hate flying, as does Ralph Coates. At least the journey was not too long and soon we were at Old Trafford facing such legendary names as George Best, Bobby Charlton, Denis Law, Nobby Stiles and Brian Kidd.

Playing towards the Stretford End, we started to put pressure on United. I managed to squirm around a couple of defenders and whack the ball with my left foot past Alex Stepney. We were one up against Manchester United and I'd got the goal. Christ. Now I know for sure I am going to get kicked.

Of course, we were bombarded for the next 60 minutes by all those brilliant players and during that onslaught we conceded two goals. But in the last couple of minutes we managed to win a corner. Cliffy Jones crossed the ball which was flicked on at the near post and I smashed it into the roof of the net. I was engulfed by my teammates and we trotted back to the halfway line as slowly as we could. Suddenly we realised the linesman was waving his flag with the home crowd baying for offside. The referee, with Dave Mackay close on his heels, sprinted across for words. He turned and pointed to the centre spot. God, what a relief. The final whistle blew almost immediately.

We had pulled off the most fantastic draw and I'd scored twice at Old Trafford. This third good game of mine in a row gave me the belief that I really could be a big part of this Tottenham side and that my decision to come to London had been the right one. The replay produced a 1–0 victory for the Spurs after extra time. This was a real ding-dong match, physical beyond all imagination. In the second half, Joe and Brian Kidd were sent off for a tussle in the Spurs penalty area. The game went to extra time and the match was settled by a goal from our winger, Jimmy Robertson. The United players felt that it should not have been allowed. They said Mike England had impeded their goalkeeper, Alex Stepney.

The games came thick and fast. We played Sheffield United and I scored another thunderbolt from 30 yards. Afterwards the Sheffield United players asked me, "Do you ever tap in goals 'cause every time you come to Sheffield they seem to fly in from 30 yards out." We beat Southampton 6–1 and I scored. I did celebrate because it wasn't a damaging goal for them. Afterwards, I went see the Saints boys in their dressing room to catch up. Terry Paine nodded to me, "You're in a great outfit here; you'll do well. You made the right decision, you couldn't say no to the move." Ted Bates was his usual analytical self, pondering the game and the team's performance but he wished me well.

I celebrated my 23rd birthday with a couple of goals against Newcastle and their partisan supporters loudly clapped us off the field. We had just played some of the best passing football ever in front of them on a lovely sunny day in April on a bumpy dry ground and they were graceful enough to show their appreciation. I've always respected the Geordies: they are fantastic in their love of good football.

CHAPTER SIX

WRITTEN OFF WITH INJURY

At the end of my first season at Spurs I thought, "I have got to strengthen myself up." The pitch at the Lane was murder. Also, I had to get my life in order. Going to a strange club, living in a hotel, it is not at all conducive to a settled life and being able to play football. I was nomadic and I didn't feel comfortable. After all, coming from Southampton to London had been a real culture shock. I was still a ploughboy with a heavy Hampshire accent. And I was also quite naive. For example, whilst travelling with Bobby Moore and Alan Ball after an international get-together in which I had played for the under 23s and they for the full national team, they surprised me with an invitation to go out with them for a drink. My watch said eleven o'clock. I responded innocently, "Is there anything open now?" They fell about laughing and replied "Chivvy, the evening is only just starting – just you wait and see, ploughboy." But I was a quick learner.

Bill Nicholson always encouraged new players to buy houses in or around the training ground at Cheshunt but I bucked the trend and bought a three-storey town house in Epping for £9,700, about ten miles away. The club had put me in touch with an estate agent who introduced me to this new development which Carol and myself fell in love with. It was a bit of a schlep but Alan Mullery and Phil Beal lived even further away in Worcester Park and Redhill respectively. I must have been earning about £100 a week but I didn't think I was rich. I was on the road to being comfortable and a bit better off, even affording a holiday in Portugal.

After six weeks off doing nothing, pre-season training for the 1968/69 season was a real shock. Eddie Baily's voice alone was a shock to the system. Eddie was Bill's right-hand man, an ex-Spurs player in the famous push-and-run team, a rough and gruff man who acted tough. Eddie was the one who had to wear all the different hats, liaising with the players on Bill's behalf. "Kick, bollock and bite" was his motto. You could hardly call him a subtle man. From the very first day he made it clear he thought I was a lazy bastard and we grated from that moment on. It was only much, much later on that I started to realise he was doing it for my own good.

On the first day of pre-season training at Cheshunt

Bill Nicholson announced, "We are going for a walk." We set off at a blistering pace. Bill loved walking and he was still fairly fit in those days so he would set the pace which was about six miles an hour. I stupidly enquired how long it was going to take us. He grunted at me, "About an hour."

"An hour, at this pace, shit," I whined to the others and continued to whine all the way.

"I've never done this before," I kept telling everyone. Bill explained that you use more muscles walking than you do running and you do not suffer from impact on the hard pavements. It was then that I discovered this six-mile walk was just a warm-up! The afternoon brought more agony with circuit training and exercises. We were screaming out for a ball but it was not allowed to appear for at least two days.

The following morning we were offloaded into the hinterland of Hertfordshire and told to run back to the training ground. We tumbled off the coach laughing and joking, everyone relating their summer holiday stories. Now, there were always some who were desperate to impress, particularly the new boys. However, I certainly was not one of those. They set off hell for leather and soon disappeared from view.

I settled into a small pack consisting of Phil Beal, Cyril Knowles and Jimmy Greaves. We ran at a more sensible pace which allowed us a good chat amongst ourselves. Because we were enjoying ourselves in such a manner, after about three miles we began dropping further and further back from the main body of runners until we were completely alone.

Just then a lorry came slowly past and Greavsie jokingly thumbed it down. The next thing we knew the lorry had stopped by the kerb. Jim, who was always ready for a laugh, jumped into the back and we all clambered aboard after him. We were in our Spurs training kit so we immediately laid down low so that when we inevitably drove past the others still running on the road, they did not spot us. We only raised our heads to give directions to this kind and sympathetic driver. As we neared the training ground and turned a convenient corner we all leapt out giggling like schoolboys and praying we'd get away with it. The players now behind us must have wondered, "Where the fuck did they come from?"

Eddie Baily was waiting, stopwatch in hand, as we entered the ground. He did a complete double take as we trotted smartly past him with hardly a bead of sweat on our brows. Believe it or not, nobody split on us. That was Jim, he got away with everything.

Aches and pains are a part of football especially pre-season. In fact, in this first week of training I personally could hardly climb the stairs and had to shuffle down on my backside. My left knee began to hurt and make me wince in shooting practice as I took the weight onto it to strike the ball with my right foot. It got so bad I was forced to report it to Bill Nick who sent me to see a specialist called Mr Wilson (nicknamed Ginger because of his hair) at Stanmore Orthopaedic Hospital. He really did not find a lot wrong except for a small thickening below my kneecap.

At that time cortisone injections were the answer to everything and he gave me one. After a few weeks, with the season now started, I could not feel any improvement and was sent back to Mr Wilson again. He gave me another cortisone injection just below my kneecap. I struggled through the pain but it was really affecting me and I didn't play brilliantly for ten games. The thing is, I only felt the injury when I planted my left foot down to strike the ball. I could still run and play a game. Unlike players today, you were expected to play even if you were only 75 per cent fit, plus you were always looking over your shoulder at the next guy wanting your place.

On 21st September against Nottingham Forest at home with half an hour to go, I went to lay off a ball with my right foot. The next thing I knew I had collapsed in a heap on the ground. I looked down at my left leg and I couldn't see any kneecap. Instead I could only see a hole where it should have been. There was no pain but with my leg bent I suddenly noticed a lump up on my thigh. I put both hands on this lump and tried to straighten my leg instinctively, slowly pushing the lump down which I had realised was my kneecap. The strangest thing was that there was no pain. Jimmy Greaves was the first to reach me and said, "Come on big fella, up you get."

"I can't Jim," I said, "I can't move. I have got a real problem here. My knee has gone."

"Fuck off, your knee can't go," he replied. Everyone crowded around and then Cecil Poynton arrived by my side. With my leg straight out in front of me, Cecil knelt down and asked me to bend it.

"I can't," I told him.

"Just try it slowly," he said encouragingly. As I gingerly started to bend my leg, my knee cap started to ride up the front of my thigh. The players around me instantly turned away and John Pratt was nearly physically sick at the sight.

Cecil put on a splint to keep my leg straight and secure and by this time four old Johnnies from the St John's Ambulance Brigade had arrived with a stretcher, having left the trolley on the sideline. They must have been 70 years old apiece.

I manoeuvred myself onto their stretcher and they heaved and panted their way to the tunnel. I was thinking this was no way to leave the ground when the old boys came to a confused halt at the top of the tunnel. In front of them were a dozen steps. Apologetically one of them asked me very nicely "Excuse me Mr Chivers, can you hop off while we get the stretcher down and then you can hop back on at the bottom." Not only was I too heavy for them but I would have slid off the front of the stretcher if they had tried to take me down.

"No problem," I said and duly got off the stretcher,

hopping down the steps on my right leg and then getting back on the stretcher as requested at the bottom. Fortunately for me, Tottenham had just that season organised a link up with the Royal Orthopaedic Hospital with an ambulance and emergency police escort now available if needed. With sirens ringing round the North Circular, I was whisked off to the hospital before the final whistle had blown.

Spurs did have a resident doctor who the players only wanted to see before the game, because by the end of it the alcohol level in him would be a little too high for any kind of accurate prognosis. He was a real character, someone who all the players liked and enjoyed a bit of a joke with. He gave us red pills, blue pills, white pills, big pills, small pills: we did not have a clue what we were taking. He told me every one of them was for pain.

By the time I'd got to the hospital the pain had kicked in and my knee was X-rayed. After establishing that I had had a cup of tea at half time, the operation I needed had to be postponed for at least two hours until about eight o'clock. The surgeon to operate on me was called Mr Trickey. Ginger Wilson was on his way back from Manchester and would join in and assist midway through the operation, which lasted four hours. When I woke up I discovered what had happened.

Basically, the two cortisone injections I had been given in pre-season had been put into the patella tendon which holds your kneecap in place. We now know that cortisone should never be injected into tendons: it's absolutely taboo. I had been a bit of a guinea pig. The cortisone had softened the tissue below my kneecap and the tendon had just snapped. I was lucky that a few fibres of the tendon were still attached and, having drilled the kneecap, they were able to introduce artificial tendons to the remaining few to strengthen the whole structure. Mr Trickey put in 50 micro-stitches to hold the tendon to the patella and I finally had 16 great big carpet stitches around the front of my knee.

It was the first time I'd had a serious operation and the first time I had been given an anaesthetic lasting such a long time. I was as sick as a dog in the recovery room after theatre and continued to be violently sick all night. The next day Bill Nick arrived with Doc Curtin and the specialist. They all wore very glum faces. Honestly and very matter-of-factly, Bill told me, "Listen Martin, you have got a problem. You've had a very bad injury and all I can tell you at this time is that you are going to be out of football for at least six months."

Six months was obviously the healing period and as it was such a rare injury none of them knew the prognosis for the future. He said, "It's all very unfortunate; we are all very sorry; we just wish you all the best," and he left. He had never once said anything about "*When* you get back."

The ward was full of guys with their legs in plaster hanging in the air by ropes and pulleys. Their injuries were mainly from motorcycle accidents where they had broken their femurs. All of them were in traction and I really did not feel so badly off in the ward with them. One of the boys had been there for 38 weeks but they all knew who I was and tried to cheer me up as I was groggy for days. Carol and my daughter Andrea at least helped me realise that I still had my family.

The same day that Bill was with me, a male nurse came to ask permission for three Spurs supporters to be allowed in for a couple of minutes to wish me all the best. "I don't mind," I said, "so let them in but I am not up to much talking." Three young Spurs mad supporters sat with me for only a few minutes and it was only many years later that I realised just who had come in specially to see me. Irving Scholar, who later became chairman of the club, and his two friends Malcolm Westbury and Gary Frankell were the first to wish me a speedy recovery. I have never forgotten that gesture to this day. I think it was typical of such a great football club's support.

After a week I was moved to Great Portland Street, the other section of the Royal National Orthopaedic, and after another week I was allowed to go home. The funny thing was that I wasn't at all worried, I never once thought that this was an injury that could put me out of football forever. But everyone else did. Two years after the injury I was playing golf with Doc Curtin. He confided, "You know you were written off, don't you?" I told him that I had no idea. "They didn't think you'd ever play again. Spurs had been in active negotiations with their insurance company, that's how convinced they were that you were finished."

The rehabilitation was very difficult because I'm a really active person, a doer. I don't read books or watch much TV but I couldn't do anything because of this bloody great big plaster on my leg. After about four weeks it was driving me crazy. I was getting this terrible itching in the whole leg. Itching, itching, itching. I stuck talcum powder down there, I tried to probe it with a knitting needle just to scratch it but nothing worked. I complained so much to the doctor at Tottenham that he sent me to the Royal National Orthopaedic Hospital in Stanmore where they got out the circular saw that they use to take plasters off. They sliced it open and to everyone's relief the area where the operation itself had taken place, which was covered in gauze, was dry. The rest of my leg from the knee down and from the top of the knee up my thigh was red raw and weeping. They realised that I was allergic to plaster of Paris. Thank God the injury was still dry and had not been affected.

What they did then was bathe it with iodine and I can tell you that stings an awful lot. But in a funny kind of way it was a wonderful feeling; it was relief that something was cleaning my leg. I spent most of the day in hospital and during that time they put a back splint on. A back splint is when they put a full plaster on your leg and then cut it in half so that the front of your leg is exposed and the back part of the leg is covered. This allowed the air to get to my leg although I was absolutely horrified at how thin it was. The fattest part of my leg was the knee. This was when I started to get really worried. "How the hell," I thought to myself, "am I ever going to build it up again?" It really was a frightening thought and one that brought home to me the seriousness of the injury.

I went home in this half splint on my crutches. I could not drive and so a neighbour took me to all the Spurs games. After two months, Mr Trickey and Cecil Poynton worked out a rehabilitation strategy for my leg. Spurs hired a car to take me twice a day to Stanmore, which is a damn long way from Epping. This process involved bending the knee slightly, a few degrees – five or ten degrees each time – in a warm therapeutic pool. Obviously I had to remove the splint each time and then it was reapplied to make sure I did not accidentally bend it too far. Mr Trickey told me I could do as many bends as I liked at home and said "it is the best exercise to build up the muscles that hold your knee in place." I used to place a rolled-up towel under my knee and then just lift the foot off the floor. It took several months to gain the flexibility to bend it to 90 degrees but even then I was unable to jog: I could only walk.

I now had a rocker fitted to the bottom of the plaster so that I could take weight on that injured leg. This made me more mobile and I began looking for things to do. In fact, I got so bored in that I decided to crazy-pave the front driveway of the house with York stone. Next door had done it so I thought why not keep up with the Joneses? I could manoeuvre the wheelbarrow, mix the cement and lift the stones. In hindsight it may have been a damn stupid thing to do: I could have tripped or fallen and set the whole healing process back months, but it kept me occupied. Once when I was walking down the three flights of stairs with Andrea in my arms I tripped and my leg with the plaster took out the entire balustrade. However, the leg was not damaged. Far more importantly, nor was Andrea. It really was one of the most stupid things I have ever done.

Just before Christmas, with all this going on in my life, tragedy struck. On returning home from one of these sessions, Carol took me into the sitting room and told me that my dad had just had a massive heart attack and died very suddenly waiting in the queue to clock off at work. It was completely out of the blue. He was only 59. OK, he did smoke, like all men of his age, but he was also a big, strong and fit man, steady as a rock, head of the family. I had the most enormous respect for him. Although he was not affectionate or tactile towards me, he had been the provider and given the family all that it needed.

Fortunately, he had seen me play a few games for Tottenham before he passed away, and score a few goals too, which allowed him to go to work with his head held high. Sadly he never saw me play for England at

Wembley or win any cups. That was my dream and may well have been his. But I will never know. It was such a sad and bad time. At the funeral itself I was hobbling around, looking after my mum. Thankfully I had Tom, my older brother, who shared the duties and helped me get through it. When I eventually did play at Wembley for England and scored goals, I always thought about Dad and how I wished he had been there to see me.

Life had to go on and although I realised I was still grieving quietly, it was important to get on with things. In that chest-high therapeutic pool, I got my leg past 90 degrees to 125 degrees over the course of five months. Trickey said not to worry about never getting to full bend – 130 degrees – I would still have the ability to do everything I needed to do. I was still very concerned about the thinness of my thigh.

Weight training at the ground with Cecil Poynton and Bill Watson, who was the British Olympic Weightlifting champion, now began. In his book *Football Fitness*, Bill Watson wrote about me, "All the confidence had drained from him and the slow build-up to mental and physical fitness was quite a process." He was also the one who started the name 'Fairy' for me – not, I assure readers – for any reason other than my "featherweight action for a man with big shoulders like those of a heavyweight boxer".

I spent a lot of time in the treatment room with Cecil. He had started at Tottenham way back in the

'50s and would tell me his stories again and again. He received a lot of mickey-taking from the players as they took their turns on his treatment table. He could make mistakes like treating the wrong leg and the player in question would say nothing for ages. But his forgetfulness was the most entertaining thing for us. One day he was sent by Bill to get some studs and strappings from the sports shop down the road. He duly went off in his car and returned with all his purchases for the afternoon session. When he came to lock up at five o'clock as normal, he could not find his car. In a panic, he called the police to report it had been stolen. Of course, it hadn't been stolen. He'd left it outside the sports shop.

Cecil and Bill Watson worked me hard. Those two men had me jumping through hoops for them, literally. Some of their techniques were unbelievable. Bill had me weight training in the morning and in the afternoons, while Cecil made me carry him on my back up and down the terraces. They were bloody big terraces at Tottenham. I would hold onto the crash barriers and do squats with him still on my back. He would then have me running round the track and that's when I set the record for the fastest time around the track that runs round the White Hart Lane pitch, 47 seconds. Nobody has ever beaten it.

Other exercises included holding weights in my hands and jumping to avoid moving poles, weights strapped to my head for neck strengthening, press-ups with the full weight of Bill on my back and endless sit-ups. Towards the end of the season I was getting really fit, reporting every two months to Mr Trickey hoping all the time that he would let me kick a ball. The team were due to go to America at the end of the season and I thought, "At last I am going to get to go away with the team" but no, he made me stay at home. I had missed the whole 1968/69 season.

It wasn't until pre-season training for the 1969/70 season that I kicked a ball again. I started with some apprehension because I had not tested my leg in any way. I was a bit reluctant to go into a tackle and go for the ball. My confidence needed to be built up and I seemed to be holding back, not determined enough to win the ball in and around the goalmouth. I had been assured the strength was there in my leg but it was obviously not in my mind. That season I had a tough time trying to regain some of the confidence I had prior to my injury. I simply didn't have the aggression to get the ball and go at the opponent.

The fans appreciated I had had a bad injury and they just kept quiet and were patient with me. Although I was able to score against teams like Arsenal and Manchester United, I knew that I was not firing on all cylinders. It was a frustrating time. I somehow had to be convinced that my knee was going to survive a tough tackle.

This was still not enough for Bill. He was trying everything he could with me. Unknown to me he talked with Mike England and Peter Collins before a training match. He instructed them to rough me up to get some reaction and stir up some aggression in me. It worked. After a continual bombardment of tackles from behind from the pair of them, Mike England kicked me up in the air and I lost it. I went hell for leather for him and kicked his legs away. A real scrap ensued and we had to be pulled apart. Bill's retort was to demand what the hell I was doing – I could have broken Mike's legs!

I think that the lack of aggression in my personality may stem from my childhood and my family who were easy-going people. I had a wonderful childhood. There were no aggressive people around the area, no gangs with knives and guns, and I rarely got into any trouble. Even at school no one picked on me. I never got involved in fights. I simply was not an aggressive person by nature. But Bill Nick really felt that I would be a much better player if I had some of Bobby Smith in me. As far as big strikers go, Bobby Smith was my true predecessor at Spurs. He played in the Double-winning side and he was very successful for the club, scored a lot of goals. But he was a completely different player to me. He put himself about and Bill wanted me to have some of that aggression. I found it very hard. It is not in my nature and I don't think you can put that into anyone's nature unless you start whacking that person and then you might get a reaction which is what Bill laid on that day.

Other teams picked up on this side of my character.

After I retired from football, the great Leeds defender Norman Hunter once said to me, "Thank Christ you never lost your temper. Teams were frightened that if I lost my temper I would be impossible to play against." But my only aim was to score goals. That was my job and to get that job done I had to play football my way. For example, say I was receiving the ball near the opposition's goal and I had a defender breathing down my neck. I would rather keep my eye on the ball, flick it away, turn and then get my shot in at goal rather than challenge that defender. I didn't want to challenge because of my size. If I challenged in the way Bill wanted it would be a foul against me every time.

My attitude was that as long as I was scoring goals I was doing my job. Bill didn't see it that way. He and Eddie always said I was aloof and very stubborn. They also thought I was very moody but the only time I was moody was when I wasn't scoring goals. In his autobiography *Glory Glory* Bill said that I was a "proud and insular man". He said that if he had a row with Jimmy Greaves, for example, the next day Jimmy would come into training all chirpy and the argument was forgotten. But I am not a chirpy man. I was trying to do my best for the football club and I wanted to score goals. If I didn't score I would sit there afterwards and put myself through the ringer. I would think, " I missed that chance and I could have done better here and so on." And that would go on until the next game when I could make up for it and hopefully score a goal. I was a perfectionist but I never got angry on the pitch.

I rarely got booked in games but after a purge by the FA in 1971, new rules were brought in for the referees. In three consecutive games I managed to get three yellow cards because of these changes. One was for not standing ten yards away from the ball and the other two were given for not taking a free kick quickly enough after the referee had blown. In one case, I had been standing there innocently waiting for Martin Peters to run over the ball and leave me to hit it. This was just one of our many pre-rehearsed free kicks. Unfortunately, Peters stood still and I got booked for not playing the ball. I was hauled before the FA. Bill Nick accompanied me. The FA fined me £25 but there was no ban. As we left the building, I looked up to Bill and said, "I expect the club to pay that."

Overall, I was always very respectful of refs. Again, this probably goes back to my childhood. If the police came round, we took notice of them. Officialdom was something that I respected and never questioned

I might not have been aggressive but I was quick. On one occasion Bill Nick brought together all three groups of players – first team, reserves and juniors. He lined all of us up across the field on the goal line. Typically he stood behind us with his whistle and we had to sprint to the edge of the penalty area so Eddie could see who was first. We repeated it to the halfway line and again Eddie wrote down the results. Finally we ran the whole length of the field. I won the first two and came second to Pete Collins over the longer distance. I don't know whether I proved Bill and Eddie wrong or right but it caused a bit of a stir as the rest of the players could not believe I was so fast.

Even so, Bill Nicholson was still frustrated. He had been reassured by the specialist that my knee was as strong as before even though I had lost muscle bulk. Therefore, he could not understand why I seemed so apprehensive on the pitch.

If I had a poor game he would ask me how many shots I had had on target. I replied with three. He said, "Three shots in a game? That's not good enough. It's all right you pulling wide to make space for yourself but when the ball is anywhere around the penalty area you've got to get in there, you've got to break your neck to get in there."

He would also tell me, "Don't be frightened to shoot through players' legs. You'd be amazed at how many goals are scored through players' legs: all you need is the slightest deflection. You can't always have a picture-book goal: sometimes it will come off your arse, your knee, but it is still your goal. Take it, get the first touch."

He always preached that I should shoot across the goal, forcing the goalkeeper to make a save. He said it might then drop down for one of the others to tap in. We practised free kicks and crosses monotonously under his instruction until our heads ached from heading those big, heavy leather balls. There was also my long throw which got enormous attention on the practice field.

He never got complicated with the moves he coached. For example, a simple 30-yard ball would be played up from the halfway line, in the air or on the ground, and I would have to meet it before the centre half and either lay it off or keep control of it. I had to be on my toes and work hard at this exercise because the centre halves were as keen as mustard to stop me.

One Saturday, as the season was coming to an end, Bill Nick took me aside and said "You're not playing today – here are two tickets for West Ham. I want you to go and watch Geoff Hurst." What a fucking insult. I'm a top player, you bought me for a record fee and you're telling me to go and watch Geoff Hurst. I was a bit embarrassed as all the players knew what Bill had done. It was a bit like suddenly asking Mike England to go and watch Bobby Moore. I thought I was a better player than Geoff but of course Bill wanted me to play like Geoff Hurst played, the way he came off defenders so that he could receive the ball, the way he ran off the ball creating space for his teammates.

Another thing I noted while sitting in the stands at Upton Park was that Geoff always made himself available to receive the ball out of defence, whether it be on the left or the right. Having seen him I really did try and start playing a bit like that. Bill must have known what he was doing as it does anyone a world of good to watch another player and learn something from them. To be fair it did seem to help me turn a corner after that.

Another important thing to come out of West Ham and over to Tottenham was one of their World Cup winners – Martin Peters. The transfer deal involved Jimmy Greaves going in the opposite direction. This was an enormous surprise to all the players and the supporters because Jimmy was an icon in the team but had recently lost form. Martin Peters was also instrumental in helping me turn that corner and we gradually began to build up a terrific understanding on the football field. He was the major influence in turning me into the player I became for Spurs.

In pre-season 1970/71 Bill Nick, in all his wisdom, took us to Majorca to play some friendlies. On arrival, sussing out what we were doing that night became the most important thing for us. On one of the first nights there, my roommate Roger Morgan had a couple of drinks, fell down the steps of the club we were coming out of and twisted his ankle. He was sent home the very next morning.

We were set to play a tournament in the big stadium in Majorca with quite a few Spurs supporters coming to watch. We were not due to play until the second day so most of the time was spent messing about in the pool taking the piss out of CSKA Sofia who were sat inside listening to team talks.

The whole tour had an air of casual fun about it. We sauntered along to the stadium about an hour and a half before the first game started, having not been told anything about a grand opening ceremony. To our surprise over the tannoy they officially started to announce the teams. Out marched FC Cologne across the running track with their green-and-white tracksuits with FC Cologne blazened across their backs. Atlético Madrid were then announced and they smartly stepped out to line up in their red and white followed by CSKA Sofia.

Then came Tottenham Hotspur. First of all, there were only nine of us instead of the 16 and we were all in different parts of the stands. Some of the players were still in the seats chatting up some birds and the rest of us were gathered in a heap alongside the track. We were a motley crew dressed in flip-flops, odd shorts and T-shirts. We hesitantly strolled across to line up on the pitch facing the crowd – hardly a professional presentation.

FC Cologne were our first opponents and unknown to me, Martin Peters and their player Overath had been arch-enemies since the 1970 World Cup. While we were playing all I could hear was Martin saying "they're taking the piss," and the next thing I know Martin whacked Overath, who retaliated. They both got sent off. Cyril Knowles then decided to carve someone up and another red card followed. We eventually lost 1–0. That meant we had to play the next day but CSKA Sofia had won their game and so now they were waving to us from the swimming pool.

Needless to stay we got stuffed by Atlético Madrid. So the summary from our Majorcan pre-season trip was two players sent off, one sent home and both games lost. Still, I got a lovely suntan.

I started the 1970/71 season with a goal every two games. However that still wasn't enough for Bill or Eddie Baily. I was still not playing up to their expectations. I was as frustrated as they were. Although I was scoring goals, I knew deep down inside that my performances were not as I knew they could be. I was desperately trying to prove my worth, not only to Bill and Eddie, but to myself. There was still more to show and only I knew that I could do it. Bill and I were becoming uptight with each other. Tensions were running high. Furthermore, my fear was that the fans would start treating me the same as they had done to previous players who had not come up to scratch in their eyes. You've got to do something very special at Tottenham to give them the belief that you're back and capable of achieving great things.

For me, as I've already explained, that happened against Stoke City at White Hart Lane. My first-half goal, the one where I barged Dennis Smith off the ball, ran from the halfway line and curled my shot past Gordon Banks, had me on cloud nine only for Bill Nick to bring me back down to earth in the dressing room. That day he really disappointed me and I started to wonder what on earth I had to do to please him. Our turbulent relationship was becoming increasingly obvious to all the players at the club. Mullers had stood up for me and to this day I still have terrific respect for the way he looked after me at half time that day.

That season, Leeds were the formidable team in the division, having played 16 games without defeat by the time we met them. Skilful and physical, every one of their players knew how to look after themselves. The instructions from Bill that day were to "jockey the goalie – Gary Sprake – make him kick with his dodgy left foot."

I did exactly what he said and it was a painful experience to my privates as Gary followed through after kicking the ball. God, that hurt. It was the only time a kick brought tears to my eyes. They were all over us from the start and only a great display by Pat Jennings and a lot of luck kept us in the game. We only had three chances at goal in the entire game and I scored with two of them. That 2–1 win halted their run. Someone said it was like stealing the crown jewels, as I was the only Spurs player to venture into their half. We departed the pitch and ground very sheepishly.

Of course Bill was highly critical of our win. He was as honest as ever and told us we were dead lucky. Often after a game such as that Bill would tell us that we should give our win bonus to the fans. We had not earned it. My relationship with Bill had not changed at all. He was still highly critical of me. Why he couldn't praise me or pat me on the back was a constant source of frustration.

However, it was in the League Cup that we really shone that season. In the quarter-final we drew Coventry who had two very tough centre halves. Between Jeff Blockley and his fellow defenders, I expected to get kicked to kingdom come. Those guys took no prisoners. Yet in a game played on a wet heavy pitch at home, I hit a purple patch and bagged a hat-trick, with all my goals flying into the top corner of their net.

In the semi-final on a rainy evening, we played Bristol City away. For a lower division team they played very well and frightened the living daylights out of us. Our saviour was Gilly, who equalised to give us the advantage heading into the second leg. The home game proved just as difficult but, unusually, I scored from a corner and we won 2–0 to win through to the final.

My mum came up to London to see me on 27th February 1971 – my first Wembley appearance. It was an unforgettable day. We stayed at the wonderful Mayfair Hotel in London. Bill Nick had made it a tradition to stay there since winning the Double ten years previously. His team talk was thorough, going through our opponents one by one. He and Eddie Baily had watched Third Division Aston Villa closely, although we obviously did not know much about them.

I went to bed that night thinking about their centre half. Is he left-footed? Is he right-footed? Is he fast? Is he slow? How can I get the better of him? Is he good in the air? Can I lose him for pace? I told myself, "Remember to move him about because if you don't move him about you're not going to get any space." Eventually I got to sleep.

The next morning we went for a walk around Bond Street and bumped into Terry Wogan, who wished us the best of luck. Naturally all of us were very nervous as we climbed on the coach to go to Wembley. We had heard so much and seen so many pictures but driving up Olympic Way and approaching the twin towers with all the fans made shivers go down my spine. I began praying that I wouldn't let down those Spurs fans down who were surrounding the coach.

The dressing rooms were enormous and the walk through that great big tunnel to the pitch was unforgettable. I'm so disappointed that the new stadium has the players unceremoniously coming out on the halfway line, as well as the winners having to disappear from view to reappear to collect their medals.

We went to check the famously immaculate Wembley turf only to find it cut up, still suffering from the Horse of the Year Show that had been held there recently. From the dressing rooms we could hear faint murmurings and shouts but as we gathered in the tunnel the noise level from the chanting of the crowd got louder until we started that walk. Every footstep you took the level of sound increased. It finally hit us at the end of the tunnel. The intensity of the roar of the crowd was thunderous. You almost swayed back on your heels. We lined up in front of the royal box and the Duke of Kent came to shake each of our hands with a nod of the head. We just wanted to get on with it.

We had no warm-ups back then. We had two

minutes of kicking the ball to each other to gauge the feel of the surface. I always took a shot at Pat Jennings and prayed that at least one would go past him as that was a good omen for me. I always made sure one went in even if he wasn't looking. Once the whistle went, the noise of the crowd disappeared, replaced by the game and your concentration.

It took us ten to 15 minutes to get the feel of the game, to judge the speed of the ball and the weight of the pass. Because we were the favourites, the pressure was all on us. In fact, they played the better in the first half and we only managed two speculative shots on goal. I was aware that they saw me as the danger man because they had two men marking me. But in the second half we got into our stride and I got the goal every kid dreams about. Jimmy Neighbour took a shot, the Villa keeper parried and the ball dropped down right in front of me six yards out from goal. I was so very careful to keep it down, side-footing it low and hard into the back of the net. I didn't want to scoop that ball over the bar. I was aware that a defender was coming across fast to try to put in a block so accuracy was paramount. Thankfully, I got it right. My arms went up as I turned to run back towards Jimmy and Gilly, with the blue-and-white masses behind that goal erupting. For once in his life our centre back, Phil Beal, came over the halfway line to congratulate me and I said, "What the fuck are you doing here, Bealey?" He had never run that far before in a match and never did it again.

Believe it or not, I was still a bit dissatisfied with that goal because it was nothing special: it was too easy; any one of our guys could have scored. But it was a goal in a final at Wembley and I accepted it. Jimmy Neighbour, at just 20, had just come into this first team having come through the Tottenham youth system and he must have been thrilled to be playing out there. We all knew of his great ability to dribble and run with the ball and he was a popular lad too: amiable chap and always a gentleman. Sadly and much too early he passed away in April 2009.

With that goal, the ice was broken and we began to dominate. After five minutes Alan Mullery found me with a 30-yard pass from the halfway line, which I pulled down out of the sky on the edge of their box. I shielded the ball, holding off two opponents and then twisted onto my left foot and drove the shot low into the corner of the net. Again, Wembley went mad and I was much happier this time.

With ten minutes to go I could have had a third. I received the ball just inside the box and shot. Unfortunately, the ball hit a defender and went past the post. The final whistle went not long after. I had come to expect only a dour face from Bill every time I came off the pitch. So it was completely out of the blue and to my enormous surprise that the first person who came up to congratulate me was him and he was beaming. A man of few words he shook my hand and said, "Well done Mart [never Martin], congratulations," and we smiled together for the photographers.

A bottle of champagne in the plunge bath was part of the Wembley tradition, along with all the silly banter, splashing and photos. Back at the Mayfair Hotel, Bill made a speech as always, but unusually he gave me special praise saying, "I never make special comment about any player as you all know, but I feel I have to today. I'd like to congratulate Martin Chivers, not only for scoring two goals but to come back from such an horrific injury and I would just like to say well done to him."

To tell the truth, I was not listening because I didn't expect anything from Bill and only caught bits of the speech. I think he was just so relieved that we had won and that Tottenham had still not lost a final at Wembley. I thought, "My God, he is capable of praise," but he never did it again.

Morris Keston was Tottenham's number-one fan, having supported them for a hundred years! Keston was in the clothes game and held the biggest and best parties ever. Tonight's was at The Hilton and we were all dying to get away from the official club dinner and over there. Once the club reception had finished the players zoomed off to meet a thousand friends and fans who were waiting for us in one of the Hilton suites with Morris. In that company, we all relaxed and the real drinking and partying started. I was so relaxed I forgot that I had to do an interview with Brian Moore for ITV the following morning. I did it with a massive hangover and the biggest of smiles.

CHAPTER SEVEN

THE GLORY, GLORY YEARS

By the end of the 1970/71 season I was really getting to know my teammates on the pitch. Alan Gilzean and I, in particular, had started to develop a real partnership. He was the most unlikely-looking footballer ever: bald, much older-looking than he really was and not exactly an athletic figure. But what he lacked in looks, he certainly made up for in character and skill on the football field. When Gilly wanted to make a point in training he would take on and run any of the other players into the ground. The problem was he never really wanted to make a point. He lived hard and he played hard. It is well documented that Gilly liked a drink. He drank all the time, at home or away on tours: it did not make any difference to him where he was. Although he lived hard and probably got pissed more nights than not, that man proved himself time and time again on the football field. He never let anyone down. How could you not get on with such a character? Everyone loved him. He also loved the ladies and they loved him.

One time when we were playing an away game somewhere, Bill Nick got us together and said, "You're always on the phone to your wives that you miss them and all the rest of it and then the next minute you're out at the clubs drinking. Look at this. I had a letter today from a fan saying they saw Alan Gilzean coming out of a club at two o'clock in the morning." We all looked at each other. There was silence and then someone said, "No, Bill, he was going *into* the club at two in the morning." I remember we arrived one morning at training to find Gilly fast asleep in his car from the night before. We dragged him out, smuggled him into the dressing room and put him in his training kit. We had to make sure that all this went completely unnoticed by Eddie Baily. Baily would have slaughtered him. Training normally started with two laps round the White Hart Lane pitch so we tucked Gilly in amongst us and moved off. The trouble was that Gilly, still a little drunk from the night before, would not stop yabbering away. Then on the second lap, he tripped up and landed in a big box which was used to store all the numbers for the boards that displayed the half time results. Some wise-arse shouted, "Screw him down now" as it looked just like a coffin. Luckily, he had taken all the skin off his legs and was forced to retire to the treatment room for repairs.

Gilly was a quiet, mild-mannered man and I only saw him grow horns on one occasion. It was during one of the final games of our League Cup-winning season.

Spurs were the only club to have won the Double in the 20th century but that season, Arsenal were primed to win both the league and FA Cup. Of all teams, we didn't want them to match the achievement. It was in our hands, too.

They played us on the Monday night before they played Liverpool in the cup final on the Saturday. They only needed a draw to win the title. We just wanted to stop them. The biggest mistake Tottenham made that night was that they didn't make the match all-ticket. There must have been 15,000 people outside the ground at kick-off and 60,000 inside. We were told to arrive at the game early for obvious reasons but Alan Mullery had to travel all the way across London and so did Phil Beal. They had to come from Surrey and Sussex. Mullery got stuck in traffic and had to park his car in Seven Sisters Road and walk the rest of the way. He turned up 20 minutes before kick-off, not the ideal preparation for a captain.

We tried our very best that night. We really did. It was always going to be a tight game because Arsenal had such a tough defence. Defensively, they were the meanest team going. Don Howe was their coach and his famous saying was, "if you don't let the opposition score, you get a point." And that night 0–0 suited them so they played on the break. I think Gilly had the best chance of the night, a shot from an acute angle that he put into the side netting. I can't remember getting any clear-cut chances, only scrambles inside their penalty area which they successfully defended.

However, the thing that really riled Gilly that night was the presence of Bob Wilson, the Arsenal goalkeeper. I have never known Gilly go for a player like he went for Bob Wilson that night. Basically, Gilly felt that Wilson had bought a Scottish cap. He wasn't going to get in the England side so he had found a Scottish relative and qualified for the Scottish team. Gilly – as passionate a Scot as you will ever meet – was absolutely mad about this.

Back then a new rule had recently been introduced for goalkeepers. They could not bounce the ball, but they could roll it three yards and pick it up again. Now Bob had this habit of gathering the ball, looking quickly and then rolling it into space to gain ground before picking it up and kicking it. Sure enough, as soon as Bob rolled the ball, Gilly was onto him like a rabbit. He clattered into him. He did it again and on the third occasion, he clattered into Wilson's ankle.

Then, just before the final whistle, Arsenal got a corner. Somehow, Ray Kennedy got his head to the ball in the crowded penalty area and put them in front. They went mad celebrating. We thought, "Bastards!"

Foundry Lane School, 1956, holding the shield. Mr Melling is second right next to Richard Trimby. Left in all white is Graham Shaw, the much-envied Saints mascot.

Taunton's Grammar School football team, 1960.

My very first press photo, 7th September 1962, the Friday before my debut for Southampton against Charlton.

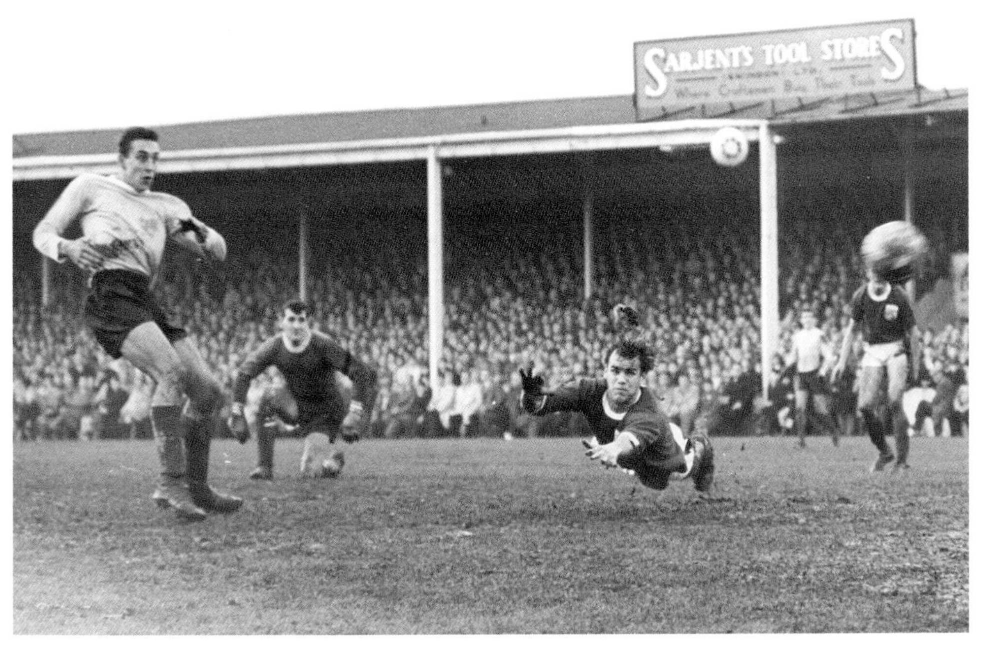

Scoring the winning goal against Swindon Town in October 1963.

Beating the great Jimmy Dickinson, facing, with a consolation goal as Portsmouth beat us 3-2 in February 1964.

Departing on tour to Malaysia, 1966. Spot the odd one out!

Scoring against Northampton in a 2-0 win in September 1964.

Terry Paine sliding in to score v Charlton. 1-0 on the way to promotion in April 1966. I am far right after an 80 yard run and cross.

Ian White, Tony Knapp and Dave Walker celebrating virtual promotion at Leyton Orient, May 1966.

Evening Standard Footballer Of the Month Award presented by Terry Paine in 1967.

Ten years old and scoring ten goals for my primary school. Cartoon by Orf in the *Southampton Evening Echo*.

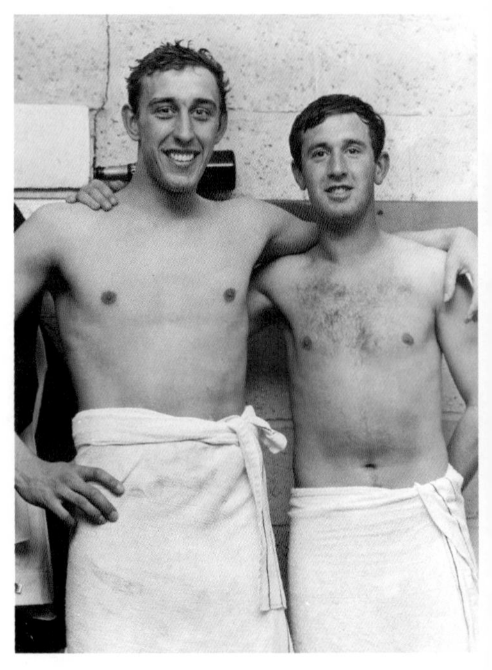

Pleased as punch with Norman Dean after our promotion winning game against Leyton Orient in May 1966.

ACTION IMAGES

British record fee of £125,000! Publicity shot after joining the mighty Spurs.

GETTY IMAGES

Joining forces with the great Cliff Jones and Jimmy Greaves, March 1968.

A close effort against my old club Southampton when I scored in a 6–1 victory, April 1968

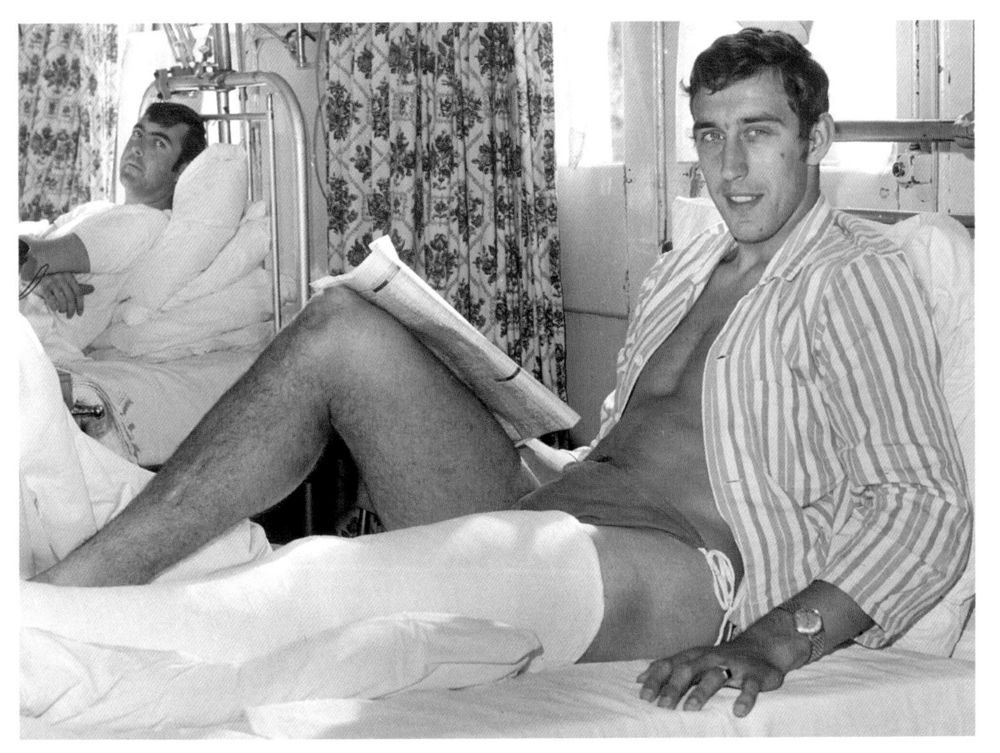

Out for nearly a year as disaster struck in September 1968 when I suffered a horrific knee injury.

ACTION IMAGES

Feeling ten feet tall emerging from the White Hart Lane tunnel to rapturous applause from the great Spurs fans. August 1969.

The Spurs cricket team, including Mike England, Eddie Baily, Phil Beal, Terry Venables, Dennis Bond, David Jenkins, John Pratt, Cyril Knowles and myself, circa 1969.

Winning the ball against Manchester City, September 1970.

PA PHOTOS

Scoring the first goal against Villa in the 1971 League Cup final.

PA PHOTOS

Cracking in the second past three Villa players in the 2-0 victory.

GETTY IMAGES

1971 League Cup final. Rare and welcome congratulations from Bill Nicholson after the final whistle.

THFC

A very proud man after receiving the Spurs Supporters Club Player Of the Year trophy, 1971.

Fresh faced and enthusiastic – myself, Martin Peters, Roger Morgan and Ralph Coates in 1972.

Recording the song, *Hot Spurs Boogie*, which never made number one on *Top of the Pops* in 1973.

Getting a shot in before being clattered by David Webb and Ron 'Chopper' Harris, League Cup semi-final 1972.

THFC

Scoring the first of my goals against Olympiakos in the UEFA Cup, October 1972.

COLORSPORT

One that didn't go in. I leap to the heavens at Molineux, 1972 UEFA Cup final, first leg.

Two that did!

THFC

Team celebrations on the pitch after winning the 1972 UEFA Cup.

We had tried our best. It was not a bad performance. I don't remember Bill having a go at us; it wasn't one of those. I think they were very fortunate to win but at the same time they never looked like losing.

After the game, Gilly and I were just walking out of our dressing room when who should pass by at the same time only Bob Wilson, hobbling on crutches with a great big bandage over his foot. Gilly's very sympathetic words to Bob were, "You big soft bastard, and you were lucky sods tonight." He was the one player Gilly grew horns for.

Our last league game of the 1970/71 season was away to Stoke. Bill was absent up the motorway signing Ralph Coates so little, rotund Johnny Wallis, who had taken over from our lovely sponge man Cecil Poynton, was in charge. He was officially the physio travelling with us, staying at hotels, getting us our newspapers and giving us our early morning calls with the words, "Does anyone want to buy a battleship?" as he drew the curtains to let in the day. He got the most terrible verbal abuse, which he took in good heart with a smile. He gave us the shortest team talk we had ever had. "We are a better team than them; let's go out and show them and make yourselves some money." Short and sweet, we went out and won 1–0 and finished third in the league.

At the end of the season we went to Japan. Personally, I never worried about having a drink the night before training because the next morning I'd just sweat it out on the track. However, on tours we were a bit like caged animals let loose. I've never in my life seen people drink as much as we did on that trip. We won all three games that we played. We beat the Japanese national team 6–0 and the club sides we beat 7–2 and 3–0. We were all six foot plus while there they were about five foot five. There's no need to explain why we took the aerial route in those games.

Bill was fine. As long as we won games, as long as we conducted ourselves on the football pitch, Bill was okay, no problem. But if results went against you then look out. His growling would get louder and louder and he would pace around the dressing room. After one game, we received a very special invitation to a sumo wrestler's house for a traditional meal. Six of us sat on our cushions on the floor, quietly respectful with our rice wine and chopsticks. We were served by lots of pretty geisha girls. Our host was the most enormous guy you will ever see, with a pretty little girl as his wife.

Gilly had not cottoned on to the fact that this girl was the sumo wrestler's wife and, low and behold, after many glasses of sake, he chose her, out of all the girls, to start putting his arms around. He took no notice of our panic-stricken glances but thank God our host was a very placid individual. He then invited us to try on his traditional sumo outfit. We all tried to look like wrestlers but Gilly, in particular, looked a complete tart.

Training the next day saw us completely wiped out,

especially Gilly, who hugged a plastic bag to himself the whole time on the coach. We had not realised the ferocity of Japanese booze. That morning Eddie put on a special session of crossing and heading which was the worse possible thing he could have done – I think he must have done it deliberately. After a dozen crosses nobody had met the ball with their head.

Eddie threatened, "If nobody heads the ball in the next six crosses we will do something you'll hate." We all stayed in our stupor and in exasperation he gave up and just put on a game. The balls were collected up and Gilly dragged a netful of them behind the goal where he promptly fell asleep. Thing is, he never got the venom from Bill that I received all the time.

I am sure Eddie and Bill's attitude towards end-of-season tours was that as long as we kept winning our games and performing we could go out and enjoy ourselves to the limit. However, on one occasion, we went over to Malta on tour and surprisingly lost a game 1–0 after enjoying ourselves a little too much the night before. Bill went absolutely bonkers. He got us in the dressing room and he barred the door by putting his hands across it and said, "Before they get you," meaning the crowd who were just as disgusted with us, "you're going to get some stick off me. That was the most embarrassing game I've ever seen. The lot of you are a disgrace to Tottenham. You were all out last night drinking away and then you go and put on a performance like that. You should be ashamed of yourselves." He went absolutely mad and he was right. He did not realise that the main culprits (who cannot be named) were not in the room at the time but were outside chatting up some girls.

Bill was never a drinker himself and his principles were so high he expected us to be the same. That said, the team were becoming a family. Steve Perryman had arrived through the youth system. He was just in his twenties, a skilful, hard-working midfielder who became the darling of the Spurs faithful and one of the club's youngest ever captains. Reputations did not impress him. However, we couldn't believe it when Bill decided to put him in with Alan Gilzean as a roommate when we played away games. We thought, "He's a blue-eyed innocent boy sharing with Alan Gilzean. Bill knows what Gilly's like." We thought he was the most unlikely roommate for Steve. Perhaps Bill thought he'd grow up a bit quicker.

My roommates changed quite a lot because I snored, so most players refused to share with me. Pratty (John Pratt) tried it and said, "Fuck that." Then Joe Kinnear and Phil Beal had a go and they all moved on to someone else. I must have roomed up with nearly every player – Mike England, Cyril Knowles, Pat Jennings, John Pratt and Martin Peters. In the end I finished up with Ralph Coates. He didn't know I snored because he was the next new boy.

Bill Nick had bought Coates in the summer of 1971 for £190,000 from Burnley. We now know it was Darkie,

Bill's wife, who made him go to look at him. She was always in love with Ralph. On Bill's instructions I picked him up at the station in his bell-bottomed check trousers and platform shoes. The famous hairstyle was slicked down and there was no wind blowing that day. His wife, Sandie, sported hot pants and knee-high white boots. They stayed with me and Carol while house-hunting and we became good mates. He turned up at Cheshunt in the same outfit and boy did he get some stick. He became the brunt of Phil Beal, Cyril Knowles and Joe Kinnear's sarcasm for all the time he played. He took it all with good humour and seemed to enjoy being the centre of the jokes, even to this day.

Bill Nick set up the team in a 4-3-3 formation with me, Gilzean and Ralph up front. The danger of playing this way was you wouldn't get enough players into the box to score. So Bill emphasised that both wide players had to follow in behind me on crosses. Ralph was not strong in the air but he still had to get into the box if Gilly was crossing the ball and vice versa. It worked like a dream in one UEFA Cup game against FC Cologne at White Hart Lane in 1973 when the ball came from the right and Ralph headed the best goal he ever scored for Spurs. I am sure Bill would have insisted that someone like David Ginola would have to get into the box on crosses. You had to get in where it hurt at all times. Although it was worth the money to watch him play, Ginola wasn't one to get stuck in and certainly did not relish the physical contact.

Another element of our partnership was that I had to anticipate Gilly's flick-ons, which he managed brilliantly off that shiny bonce. I always anticipated that he would get some form of touch on the ball and so I always strived to get on the end of it. He would never head the ball down but had such a deft touch to his flicks. Very often passes came from Martin Peters on the right for Gilly to get a touch and put it into my area. Partnerships are so important in a team and fortunately I also struck up a great link with Martin. He created so many chances for me. I had become his Geoff Hurst, always looking to take advantage of a situation, especially the ball to the near post.

Time and time again Martin would take free kicks from the right and as soon as he put his hand on the ball and stepped back two paces to play it I was off gaining half a yard on my opponent. This was all I needed to get a touch with any part of my body – head shoulder, knee, foot – and direct it towards goal. We scored so many goals like that.

This 1971/72 season became memorable because Bill Nick introduced us to Hunter Davies, who was proposing to follow us through the season and write a book. He had written one previously about the Beatles and had got the blessing of the club to do the same with us. We all thought, "Yeah, we have heard it all before." We had no idea how big it was going to be. But what a fantastic season to choose.

Initially, he wanted to get such an insight into the

team that he was going to join in with us for pre-season training. The first small-sided game that he took part in was only five minutes old when we noticed him sitting on the bank with a pen and paper in his hands. That was the end of his football initiation. It had been a bad idea. From then on we saw him everywhere with that pen and notepad – in the dressing room, on the coach, on the planes, in the hotels, everywhere. The book was given the name *The Glory Game* and was a best-seller thanks to our enormous success that season.

Personally, when it came out I thought it was a true insight of the workings of a top-class football club. Hunter gave each player a draft of the chapter about them. It's a good thing he did, because many of the players would have been divorced within five minutes if he'd published what he first wrote about them. Eddie Baily screamed when he read his chapter. He said, "I can't allow this. He makes me seem like a moron." We just looked at each other and said, "Well?" True to form, Bill never commented on the finished work.

There were parts in my chapter that I thought had been taken out of context. For example, he says in the book that I was scared to be alone. Not true. What I was saying is that when you live in a great big house and you are rattling around in it on your own you are lonely, not scared. No one would like being on their own in a great big house like that. That's why Joe Kinnear would come round now and again and we would go to Walthamstow Dog Track together. We had some good times there. He also quoted Martin Peters's wife as saying that I never gave Martin any credit for my goals. Well, you don't say those things at the time. I am doing my job and he is doing his. He wouldn't stand up then and say that for a two-year period Martin Chivers was the best centre forward in Europe, if not the world. But he does now. It is when you look back that you credit those who helped you. These days I always introduce Martin Peters at the lounge at Spurs where I work by saying that it is no coincidence that when he came to the club we started winning and I started scoring lots of goals.

I scored three goals in the first four games of the season and the team was successful in winning the Anglo-Italian Cup over two legs against Torino but it still didn't stop my manager's constant criticisms. He did not want me to get too full of myself and flex my muscles with him. He wanted full control and suppressed any praise at all. I understand that now but what I would not suffer was things like Eddie Baily screaming at people in training. We constantly got bitched at in training. Bill and Eddie would expect people to run round the track and throw up at the end of it. I have never once done that. Maybe I didn't push myself to the absolute limit but I think I gave more than enough. In the gymnasium I certainly gave 100 per cent. Along with Peter Collins and Pat Jennings, I was the strongest in the team. I could lift weights like they were flies. But ask me to do long-distance running and that was a different story.

The trouble with Bill was that he gave his everything to the club and he expected everybody else to. But it was very difficult for me to run myself into the ground in the way he did. In some matches, for instance, balls would be played over the top of the defence and be going towards the goal line. I could judge whether I was going to reach them or not and 90 per cent of the time I was right. Maybe once or twice the ball got stuck in the mud and I thought, "Oh fuck, I should have gone for that", but most of the time I was right not to chase it.

A lot of players – and I'll name one, John Pratt – used to run for lost causes. Although he rarely got the ball the crowd would applaud him. To them he was wonderful but I could have told you before he set off that he was not going to get the ball. What got Bill upset was that sometimes I would not go for a ball that he believed I could have made. He wanted to see me make an effort and when I didn't that was really frustrating for him. In fact, it would drive him mad. Bill would have made the effort but he still wouldn't have got it and that's what the difference was. Today I hate watching myself on TV or on DVDs of old games because I do look slow, I do look lazy, but all I can say is that I was trying my best. You always go out onto the football field to try your best and some days my best was not good enough. I admit that. In some games I wouldn't touch the ball for 50 minutes but that was unacceptable to Bill. He wanted you to be amazing in every game. That's what a manager has to do, try and get his players playing their very best. He just could not understand or tolerate when that didn't happen.

> *"It's true Martin Chivers scored twice but he should have had three goals . . . he is not entitled to put the ball over the bar from there."*
> **Bill Nicholson, *The Daily Telegraph*, 23rd September 1971**

A bit of a joke started around the time that every time Sir Alf Ramsey, the England manager, came to watch Spurs, I always played well. Also *The Big Match* television crew brought out the best in me scoring goals. I always had a standing joke with their great commentator, Brian Moore. He'd say, "We're here, Martin", and I'd say, "Great, I am due a goal then", very often obliging for the cameras. However, the television brought out the fact that I never smiled when I scored a goal. People constantly asked why I never smiled or celebrated. The reason was that I was too embarrassed. I did not have any teeth. It was dangerous to play with my dentures in and therefore I would only have been giving a great big toothless grin like Nobby Stiles and I was too proud for that. I would like to say that they had been knocked out in a football match. But the truth was that they had gone rotten at the age of 12 and I had been goofy since then.

Keflavik, an Icelandic team, were our first UEFA

Cup opponents. We could not have wished for an easier baptism. We coasted home 6–1. To celebrate we went out to a nightclub. We did not know that selling alcohol in Icelandic clubs was prohibited. When we got to the club we immediately realised that everyone was plastered on coke and lemonade. They had brought in their bottles in their big coat pockets and tucked them under their tables.

Graeme Souness was a young player on the fringes of the first team then and he was talking to some local people at the bar. The Icelanders all spoke good English. Some fella kept constantly poking him in the back to get his attention. He wanted an autograph. I noticed this happening. Suddenly, Graeme just spun round and poked him in the eye. He went down like a sack of spuds so I went and helped the guy up, noticing that he only had one arm. I said, "Graeme, careful this fella's only got one arm; all he wants is an autograph."

Graeme replied, "He'll have to wait, I am talking to people."

I explained to the man to be patient and that Graeme would sign for him in a minute. But he had obviously had too much to drink and started poking Graeme again and again in the back. So Souness turned around and did exactly the same thing again. You just can't win with some fans. Graeme wasn't the only one who suffered fans lightly. Pat Jennings and I got a reputation for not being very forthcoming.

I personally did not have the patience in those days

and hated it when fans did things like asking for an autograph just as I was about to put my food in my mouth at dinner. I also did not like people coming onto the pitch immediately after the game and stuffing papers or programmes under my nose. The adrenaline was still pumping, my hands were shaking and cold, they never had a pen and they expected you to write your name there and then. They could be very demanding.

For me there was a time and place for such things. After the game was not a problem when you have calmed down and they have a programme and a pen. But you've only got to refuse a few times and you get a reputation as being a stuck-up bastard with no time for anyone.

Fans could also cause other problems. On one occasion we turned up in a coach at a hotel in Liverpool and across the road stood two fellas who were giving Mike England the wanker sign. Mike was a mild-mannered man, always sociable with lots of friends as he was a great talker, but underneath he was a volcano waiting to erupt. He just could not believe these two guys were doing this to him and pointed at himself as they gestured. They nodded back. Mike jumped up, asked his roommate, Bealey, to take his bag and walked calmly off the coach and across the road. He flattened both of them and then walked back to the hotel. He did not stand any nonsense and that attitude got us into some other sticky situations.

During a very heated game at Newcastle there was

a set-to between him and Wyn Davies which saw a bit of bloodshed. After the match their fans were baying for more. The coach took us to the station after the game and as we approached the ticket control, there were about 200 of them waiting especially for Mike. As we got to the barrier, a cup of hot chocolate flew through the air and hit Mike all over his new mohair suite. You could not have done anything worse as he was a bit of a peacock. He saw red. He reached his very long arms across five deep and laid the culprit out flat. There was a deadly silence for a few seconds and then we turned tail and started to run for our lives to the train. The crowd chased us onto the platform, we got onto the train first as we were quicker than them and probably more scared, and shut the doors. Fortunately the police on the platform stopped them coming any further. Then the police came onto the train saying, "We understand one of your players has hit a supporter."

"Oh no, officer, not one of us. We would never do that – it must have been one of our fans."

Bill Nick came along as we settled down with the train pulling out of the station. "How many times do I have to tell you Mike. Keep your cool; don't lose your temper. You're representing the club."

Mike was an easy-going man most of the time, so easy-going that one Saturday he was mowing his lawn when his wife casually questioned whether he was playing a game that day. "Yes," he replied. "Why?"

"Well, it's just after 2 o'clock", she said. They lived in Broxbourne! Mike arrived in the dressing room in his grass-stained gardening gear with 20 minutes to go to kick-off. His nickname became Bungalow amongst all the players. Never to his face, because we were all cowards. We would never dare tell him we didn't think he had much up top.

I remember that we played Leeds away that season and Gilzean scored a brilliant goal in a 1–1 draw. A lot of the papers said we played some of the best football they had seen from us in a long time. We thrashed Nottingham Forest 6–1 and we also beat Ipswich 2–1, yet still Bill wasn't happy. He had a right go at us at half time in the Ipswich game and afterwards he spoke to the press.

> *"I cannot put my finger on the reasons why we should play like this but it is an understatement to say that I am not pleased."*
> **Bill Nicholson, *The Sunday Telegraph,* 3rd October 1971**

And that's after we had won. For Bill, we were winning but not performing and in his book that just wasn't good enough. We were capable of beating any team on our day but against poor opposition, we just couldn't perform. We lacked consistency in league matches and I really think it has stayed like that to this very day at Spurs. But personally, after such an up-and-down beginning to my time at the club, I began to feel I could do nothing wrong. I became aware of the fact that if I didn't play well, the team suffered. It became an enormous responsibility, a burden even, to think that one player could make all that difference. Yet I couldn't help thinking, how could one player be so important when we had such a terrific team, full of internationals who had played together for five years? And how can you be brilliant every week? You can't always be on top form. Look at Cristiano Ronaldo. He is worth 80 million pounds of someone's money but some games you don't see him at all. In other games he sets the world alight. You can't do it every game. But I guarantee he never gets the stick from his management that I got from mine, that's for sure. The Spurs fans were always terrific to me so why couldn't the manager be more forgiving?

It had begun to weigh on my mind, especially when Bill Nick's response to any poor team performance was to target me. By now I had started to feel the injustice and I began to answer back to him. I did so on the training field and in the dressing room and many times these became full-blown arguments. I didn't care. The fact was I had at last started to stand up for myself. I was scoring so many goals and doing so well that it became very clear to me that he was totally over the top with his criticisms. Plus he was only targeting me. Now I wouldn't have minded if he went around other people in the team but he never seemed to do so. It was always me but I was scoring loads of goals and I was now in the England team so I felt I could now answer back to Bill.

That said, even then I would never have denied that Bill was undoubtedly a great manager. In the FA Cup against Carlisle, he pointed out in the team talk that one of the main reasons for their success was that their captain, Stan Ternent, played as a sweeper behind the back four. This was typical of Bill's and Eddie's thorough homework in analysing the opposition. He instructed me to push onto Ternent with my marker, therefore occupying two players and giving our strikers more room to manoeuvre. It worked like a dream as we ran out 3–1 winners.

We went on to beat Rotherham and Everton. At Elland Road against Leeds, John Pratt scored a really lucky goal. I am sure he was aiming for me across the goal but to our delight it nestled into the corner of the net. Leeds scored twice though and we were out of the FA Cup.

In the League Cup we had an excellent run, reaching the semi-finals for the second year running where we drew Chelsea. We lost 3–2 at Stamford Bridge. We fought very hard only to be beaten by the shortest player in their team – Chris Garland – who headed in a corner in the last few minutes. Bill Nick was fuming afterwards. "How can the shortest player on the field get a header against you lot?" At least he could not blame me for that one.

In the second leg at Spurs, the ground was packed to the rafters which created the most fantastic atmosphere. Alan Hudson commented afterwards that it was "A game played in a wall of noise." I opened the scoring with a brilliant volley. With Ron Harris and David Webb running at me, the ball took an eternity to drop out of the sky. I was sure they were going to cream me but I just had enough time to volley it into the net before being clattered by them both. Mike England and Peter Osgood continued where they left off in the first game, with each winding the other up. It culminated in the very last minute of the game.

We were leading 2–1 when the ball went to Peter Osgood near our corner flag. Bill Nick was always saying that if an opponent has the ball facing away from goal in that sort of situation, he has the big problem and he is not a danger. Mike England forgot all that and obviously thought it a chance to clatter him. He gave away a silly free kick. From near the corner flag, Hudson mis-hit the free kick, scuffing it low and Cyril Knowles tried to clear with his right foot. He completely missed it and it slid past a surprised Pat Jennings. We had lost the tie and it was I who picked the ball out of the back of the net. You can use your own mind to imagine Bill's words after the game. Still, at least we had something to focus on for the rest of the season. We were still in the UEFA Cup.

CHAPTER EIGHT

WE'RE ALL GOING ON A EUROPEAN TOUR

We had beaten Keflavik in the first round of the UEFA Cup by a club record score of 15–1 over two legs. Next were the French team, Nantes, who Bill didn't seem to rate judging by his teamtalks. During the game, Bill never stopped screaming and shouting my name to try and get me moving, burying his face in his hands, blurting out oaths of panic and fury. His instructions were really a running commentary. Eddie kept up a continual stream of abuse about "bloody internationals". At the end of a tough 0–0 draw there was a humdinger of an argument in the dressing room between Bill, me, Mullers and Cyril.

As usual I bore the brunt of his criticisms, him blaming me for what he viewed as a bad performance, accusing me of not doing this, not doing that.

I sarcastically said, "Some poor team," only to get another volley of abuse. As with all his complaints he always referred back to past players who "would never have played like that" and the name of Bobby Smith was always rammed down my throat. It was the most heated disagreement I had experienced with Bill and Eddie.

Apart from my frustration at the situation, I was also beginning to feel lonely and isolated because of the abuse being directed towards me. I had been nurtured at Southampton which was a small, friendly club with Ted Bates at the helm. His manner with me had been entirely different and I had thrived. Bill's man-management of me resulted in constant confrontation between the pair of us, which left both of us angry and resentful. He believed I was not performing to what he thought was my best, and I was trying the hardest I could to please him with goals.

I was, and still am, a far from confrontational person and did not retaliate to tackles or abuse. But by this time I'd had nearly enough of Bill and Eddie. Some people said I was "stand-offish" and some a "gentle giant" and also "an enigma". I was none of these, but I had learnt to stand on my own from losing my dad at an early age and I never made close friends very easily. I guess you could say I played my cards close to my chest and never showed much emotion. Bill thought this was sulking and others felt that I was aloof or arrogant. I can only say that I had become more contained and I always fought my own battles with the club and with myself.

Rapid Bucharest followed Nantes (who we'd beaten 1–0 in the second leg). The Battle of Bucharest. They didn't give any impression of being a dirty side when they played against us at home and we won 3–0, but over there they were unbelievably volatile. Fortunately we were a long, long way from the crowd thanks to the running track. They kicked lumps out of us as soon as the whistle went and we finished with eight players on the treatment table after the game, me included. Gilly had to go off at half time: he was carved to bits. Jimmy Pearce came on, scored a goal, and within three minutes he was off. He went to take a throw-in and a player kicked him as he was picking up the ball. Jimmy's reaction was to pull back his fist as if to retaliate and the referee sent him off.

We got a penalty in the second half and Martin Peters stepped up to take it. As he was about to start his run-up, their national goalkeeper, Raducanu, who had acted like a complete nutter throughout the game, sprinted off his line straight for him. He was only six yards away when Martin struck the ball past the post. Amazingly the referee allowed it and gave a goal kick. Still, I managed to get some revenge by scoring from an acute angle.

After the game there were bodies lying everywhere in the treatment room and it took a long time for all of us to get patched up. We staggered onto the coach and waited for Bill and Eddie. Bill said, "Well, I have never seen a dirtier team or a more vicious attack on a team of players than that. The only thing I can tell you is that it was so bad Bucharest have refused to hand the film of the game over to the BBC."

Believe it or not, we got Arad Bucharest in the next round – same flight, same hotel but thank God not the same ground – and we beat them to go into the semi-final against AC Milan. The first leg was at the Lane. Steve Perryman was a great defensive midfielder but not known for his goalscoring skills. However, he scored both goals in the 2–1 victory. If he never scored another goal that season it didn't matter because those two great goals gave us an excellent chance of reaching the final. Bill always emphasised that he wanted 20 goals a season from the midfield trio of Perryman, Mullery and Peters. I am pleased to say that most seasons they didn't let him down.

We knew the return game was going to be a heated affair because of the Italians' reputation for pinching, spitting and gouging. The training-ground hotel was out in the wilds – no shops, no golf, no people, no nothing. The San Siro stadium towered above us as we approached for the game in our coach and, as always, we went straight out to see the state of the pitch, which was immaculate. There were already 35,000 people waiting for us inside the stadium, ready with their firecrackers which they proceeded to throw as we wandered around testing the turf. We went to get changed, crapping ourselves with anticipation at the volatility of the partisan crowd. For the first 15 minutes, the atmosphere was electric, with the noise drowning everything else. Bill Nick had asked specially for Alan Mullery to return from Fulham for these two games. He had been suffering badly from a recurring injury and was loaned to that club to get match fit. Low and behold, it was he who scored the goal that silenced the stadium. As I picked the ball out of the back of their net you could have heard a pin drop.

Now it was all hands to the pump. In the second half I had a really good chance to put the game out of their reach but pulled the shot disappointingly wide. The last 20 minutes seemed to last for an eternity. Alan Gilzean missed the game through injury and Martin Peters was put up front with me but, when we were under pressure, Martin would drop back and I would end up as the lone ranger up front, trying the hold up the ball to wind down the clock.

At one point, Phil Beal decided, in his wisdom, to cream the Italian international Bonetti while he was on the ground and all hell broke loose. Players were pushing one another, gathering around the referee, shouting. Phil had already received an earlier booking and in all the mayhem and confusion the ref showed a yellow card for that tackle to Steve Perryman instead of Phil. Knowing the situation, Steve accepted it with good grace. Towards the very end of the game, a foul gave them a penalty from which Rivera scored. We just had to pray for no more mistakes and we put all the players behind the ball. At last that wonderful sound of the full-time whistle came. We had won 3–2 on aggregate. The referee, aware of the anger and frustration of the crowd, held us in the centre circle for 15 minutes to wait for all the missiles they had in their hands to be thrown. Chaos then ensued when we tried to leave the stadium, with the coach being rocked side to side and missiles being thrown against the glass windows.

Incredibly, we actually got congratulations from Bill Nick on our return to the Milan training ground. He said, "You've made me very proud. We've got another final to look forward to. You kept your cool in a very difficult game. I realise I've brought you to a place with nothing to do, nowhere to go for a drink, so the least I could do is get you a couple of cases of champagne and they are down in reception – a bottle each."

My roommate Ralph and I got our bottles and retired to our room. "What the hell are you doing?" I asked as I watched him smuggle the champagne into his bag. "I'm going to have it when I get home," he replied. "No you bloody well are not – you're drinking it now!" I shouted back. We sat up in bed drinking from our bottles as we went through the game. After about 15 minutes I innocently enquired what he felt about the penalty decision. He responded at great length and then turned to get my response. But all he got were enormous snoring sounds. Not that Ralph is boring but the champagne and the game had taken its toll. Normally, after a night game, it used to take me hours to get to sleep: I needed to wind down for at least three to four hours. I think that's one of the reasons footballers are known for drinking heavily after matches. But what else can you do?

The only disappointment of the cup run was that we would face Wolves in the final. We wanted a foreign team but it wasn't to be. Our wives and girlfriends were also disappointed. The club had promised to pay for them to travel to the final and I don't think they were expecting a return train ticket to Wolverhampton as their prize. Both sets of players and supporters were disappointed. When the draw was made for the semi-finals and both English teams were drawn against very strong European opposition you would have put money on one of us going out. However, the strength of English football at that time was such that both English teams came through.

On 3rd May 1972, we played the first leg of the final at Molineux. After a lacklustre first half with few clear chances, Bill Nick started to lay into me in the dressing room all over again. I shouted back, "Am I the only fucking player in this team? Why is it just me again?" and I walked off to the toilets. They had become my refuge from him and Baily. I stayed there until the half time buzzer went.

As I joined the players going into the tunnel for the second half, Mike England and Phil Beal said to me,

"Come on big fella, we know what you can do, now show *them* what you can do." We went out on the pitch, and after about 20 minutes Mike England took a free kick. I don't know why Mike took it; it was usually the full back's job. The kick was just over the halfway line about 10-15 yards into their half. He hit the ball in and I got the run on the defender. I got up high and met it perfectly with my forehead and it flew into the top corner. That, for me, was a good goal and Parkes, their goalie, didn't stand a chance. I was really chuffed and it gave us real hope. Ten minutes later, though, we got mugged. The message to be alert on free kicks had been drilled in: don't lose concentration. But we went to sleep. They took a quick free kick while we were arguing with the ref. The ball diverted off Pat's leg and Phil Beal, who was behind him, couldn't stop it squeezing into the net.

Then, with a couple of minutes to go, I met a long ball from Cyril Knowles just over the halfway line. I made one effort to lay it off to Alan Mullery but it hit a defender and the ball came back to me. I was 40 yards out and in that instant I made a decision to run with the ball. There was very little time left. We were hanging on a bit but I knew that behind that goal there were thousands of Spurs supporters and if I took a shot and missed it, they would hang onto it for 30 seconds or so. The ball sat perfectly in my stride. I pulled my right foot back and made solid contact with my instep. I knew immediately that the shot was goal-bound and it screamed into the net, which bulged with the force. The goal-keeper barely moved. It was the best goal I ever scored for Spurs, and quite possibly the hardest shot I ever hit in my life. Not bad for the deciding goal in the last minute of a European cup final.

Since that night I must have met half the Spurs supporters behind the goal that evening. If anyone says they were at that Wolves game I always ask, "Were you behind the goal?"

I raised both arms in triumph and Gilly jumped on me with his normal straddle. My arms were around his waist as he was up around my shoulders. When the final whistle blew, Eddie Baily was the first to run on the pitch to congratulate me and the first to be told to fuck off. In the dressing room we all sat down, absolutely exhausted. Baily came in.

Instead of giving me the usual bollocking he said, "Chiv, you've knocked me out. I can't believe what has happened. What do you want me to do? I'll even kiss your feet." I just ignored him. Then he came over and said, "Come on, what do you want me to do?" I just kicked him away with contempt. I couldn't take that change of face. That half time bollocking he gave me? I can see now he was trying to gee me up but at the time I just thought, "Why pick on me? There are other players in this team."

The first-class train journey back to London was wonderful with the drinks flowing. After a while, John Pratt came along the carriage and asked if we thought it time to get off the train. We were having such a great time we hadn't realised we had been stopped at King's Cross for 20 minutes.

For the return game at White Hart Lane I was a marked man and their defenders doubled up on me. The opening goal that Mullers scored was meant for me. In a planned free-kick situation Martin Peters always sent a quick ball in towards the goal for me to meet. On this occasion I started my run a split-second too early and the ball went over my head, but to my delight Alan Mullery was following in behind to score with a diving header. It was a brave header and after he made contact with the ball he collided with Parkes and lay motionless on the floor. He was groggy as I tried to pick him up but he soon came to. Wagstaffe equalised with a fantastic left-foot goal which frightened us. But despite immense pressure, Pat Jennings was on top of his game and made some amazing saves. We hung on to win the UEFA Cup.

After receiving the trophy and medals, we did a lap of honour for the crowd but Mullers wanted to go round again, being the captain and star of the show. We said, "Fuck off Mullers, we've done it once," and proceeded to go down the tunnel. It was a heavy pitch and we were all knackered. Mullers wasn't. He went off on his own for a lap of honour and the crowd on the pitch lifted him onto their shoulders and carried him round. He had come back from injury and that loan to Fulham to win the cup for Spurs. Little did we know that this would be his last game for Spurs. For me, he had been a pleasure to play with and one of the club's best ever captains. He had taken over the reins from Dave Mackay and held his own which was a feat in itself. He was always full of enthusiasm, had great skill and scored fantastic goals.

In the dressing room we filled the cup with champagne but there was no sign of Bill. Ten minutes later he came in and said, "I just thought you lot would like to know that I've just been in the Wolves dressing room telling them that the best team lost tonight." We were dumbfounded but privately thought, "What an honest bastard." That was just like him and it was not the first time he had done it. "Never mind that Bill, get a drink of this," someone said.

We knew they had been the better team on the night but we had been the better team up at Wolves. We didn't win the League Cup semi-final against Chelsea after being the better team, but that's football. Some you win, some you lose: just enjoy the moment when you do succeed. All I know is that I thought that Bill should have come to our dressing room first and then gone into see the Wolves players. But that was Bill for you.

ALAN MULLERY ON MARTIN

When he first came to Spurs I was impressed with Martin's size. He was a big powerful man, lovely build.

I had already admired him as a player when he was

at Southampton. He was always difficult to play against. He would put his arms out to defend himself and you couldn't get around him because he was so big. He also had a lovely touch, great feet.

Spurs needed someone like him at that time, we needed someone up front you could hit with a ball. Plus, he scored goals. He had proved that with Southampton and then he proved it with Spurs. In his first game he scored and we hadn't won at Sheffield in years and years. It just showed you how important he was.

If you gave Martin an opportunity to score goals, that's what he did. When Jimmy Greaves left everyone thought it that it was going to be a major problem but suddenly we had two great goalscorers in Martin and also Alan Gilzean. People did think Martin was not aggressive enough and Bill Nicholson would have been the main protagonist on that subject. On numerous occasions he was pulled off and substituted and Eddie Baily used to absolutely hammer him. I remember him screaming all the time, "Get your foot in Martin, use your strength", and at times I would feel sorry for him.

He wasn't an aggressive type of player yet he was a big man. If you were looking for aggression in that Spurs team you could look at Mike England, you could look at Cyril Knowles, you could look at Alan Mullery, you could look at Dave Mackay, and they were aggressive but also very skilful. Martin was a very skilful footballer and a strong man but he would never show that aggression. People would kick him and he would just go back for more and not say a word about it. I suppose if people don't see that then they will say he is not aggressive but he won us lots of games, and that was the difference.

The famous incident with Martin and I was during the Stoke game. He had got two goals and I was a bit late getting back to the dressing room. When I walked in Bill was absolutely ripping him to pieces. We had not played particularly well but he had scored both goals. Bill was ripping into him so I said, "Bill, for Christ's sake leave the fellow alone." Bill turned on me, "Don't you tell me what to do." He got his coat off which is what he did when he ripped into you and I told him, "Don't shout at me. I am telling you what the fellow has done." Bill gave me a shove, I gave him a shove, and now everyone is crowding into the bathroom to get out of the way which just leaves Bill and I shouting at each other.

I couldn't understand it – I never saw him to do that to Jimmy Greaves. We all knew Jimmy would score us goals and we also knew that Martin could score us goals so why he laid into one and not the other I can't give you an answer. Perhaps they felt potentially he could have been so much better. One thing I do know is that he was outstanding. He was as good as any centre forward in the country at that time.

The thing about football is this you could have your Dave Mackays, your Danny Blanchflowers, your Alan Mullerys and obviously we helped to make the side successful but the people who scored the goals, they were the people who won you games. And Martin won us games. As long as he was scoring I don't think too many players in the team were worried but the management probably expected more.

I have heard some people talk about Martin as standoffish but I never found him that way. I have always got on with him. It probably came from sticking up for him with Bill. No one else would have done that so I have an affinity with him which has lasted to this day.

THFC

UEFA Cup celebrations with Alan Mullery, Ralph Coates and Phil Beal. What a way to go for captain Mullers.

COLORSPORT

What a great partnership I had with Alan Gilzean, one that frightened so many defences. October 1972.

THFC

Can't believe this didn't end up in the back of the Liverpool net in the UEFA Cup semi-final, which we narrowly lost. April 1973.

PA PHOTOS

Wembley again for the 1973 League Cup final maintaining Bill Nicholson's record of never losing a cup final. We beat Norwich 1-0.

PA PHOTOS

Ralph Coates and I running with the cup in 1973. Ralph's goal and subsequent celebration will never be forgotten.

THFC

Scoring the first goal in a 2-0 home win against Dinamo Leipzig. UEFA Cup semi-final, April 1974.

THFC

The infamous final against Feyernoord, May 1974 – the game that marked the end of an era.

THFC

A great birthday present as I score my 100th league goal for Spurs against Leicester in April 1974.

COLORSPORT

Spurs avoiding relegation by beating Leeds 4-2 in April 1975.

GETTY IMAGES

One of my best games for England as I score twice in an emphatic 3-1 victory over the marauding Scots including Billy Bremner, May 1971.

GETTY IMAGES

Proud to be in such exalted company – Geoff Hurst, Rodney Marsh, Franny Lee and myself. December 1971, Athens.

Pass auf! Georg Schwarzenbeck gets too close in Berlin in a 1972 international.

GETTY IMAGES

The dreaded Poland match and my last appearance in an England shirt. Poland's greatest game thanks to their goalkeeper, Jan Tomaszewski. October 1973.

COLORSPORT

A welcome sponsorship deal for all the players from Honda.

In action for Servette, left is Gunter Netzer of Grashoppers Zurich.

Winning the Swiss Cup in my last game for Servette, against Grashoppers Zurich.

Hello Mum and Dad! Julia and I in Geneva holding our precious two-month-old son, Nick.

COLORSPORT

First goal of the season after returning from Servette. Norwich City v Southampton, August 1978.

Brighton rock from my daughters, Melanie and Andrea, for Teddy Maybank and myself in 1979.

HUAUGESUND AVIS

Amazed I can lift my leg this high in a game in Norway for Vard FC as the end of my career approaches.

Bill Nicholson opening our Brookmans Park Hotel which Julia and I ran for 18 memorable years. Also present, Glenn Hoddle, Phil Beal, Ralph Coates and Steve Perryman.

On holiday in Verbier, Switzerland, with my beloved family, winter 1999.

RAY PICKARD

A very proud dad as his two boys, Luke and Nick, join him in a pre-match charity game on the famous Spurs pitch.

RAY PICKARD

An enormous laugh with Glenn Hoddle, Bill, Dave Spurling and myself before Bill Nicholson's testimonial match against Fiorentina, 8th August 2001.

RAY PICKARD

Walking out onto the pitch with Bill Nicholson for his testimonial match.

RAY PICKARD

The great Pat Jennings presenting me with my award as I am inducted into the Spurs Hall Of Fame, April 19th 2007.

PA PHOTOS

I don't know who was the prouder on this memorable day! Bill Nicholson and myself acknowledging the crowd's standing ovation at his testimonial game.

OFFSIDE

Thanks for the memory.

CHAPTER NINE

HAPPY DAYS

My first league goal of the 1972/73 season came in the fourth game against Birmingham. It was always a relief to get the first goal of a season under your belt, as the longer it went on without scoring the worse things got. A striker needs to be relaxed in front of goal with no tension. I remember Jimmy Greaves going eight games without scoring which must have been a record in itself. You could see how physically and mentally uptight he was.

The team was not playing well and against Huddersfield in the League Cup we were so poor the fans started going home early. The next home game saw Cyril Knowles running towards his own goal, playing cat and mouse with the Crystal Palace winger. When Cyril had the ball and, out of the corner of his eye, saw his opponent sprint, he would sprint as well. When the guy slowed down, so would Cyril. He always had that five yards on him. This happened on a few occasions. Eventually, Cyril, sensing the winger behind him, lobbed the ball back to Pat Jennings. Unfortunately Knowlesy had not noticed Pat advancing from his goal and the ball sailed over the top of Pat's hands and into the net. Bill Nick was not too pleased.

Cyril was a natural piss-taker on and off the field. At away matches, the night before a game, we were allowed to have what we wanted for our meal. Once, in the restaurant of a Leeds hotel, Eddie Baily came in to find our table lit up with flames with the head waiter skilfully pouring on the brandy. "What the fuck are you doing?" said Eddie, to which Cyril replied, "But Eddie, you told us we could have whatever we wanted on a Friday night, and I always have Steak Diane at home."

Cyril was a classy and stylish player. He was very skilful for a full back but he could tackle hard and fast. He never seemed to panic and always played within himself. He was quite happy to dribble the ball along his own goal line rather than kick it clear. He was one of the first overlapping full backs and a major part of the success of the team. He was as cool as a cucumber but I remember he always seemed to suffer from headaches. Sadly, Cyril passed away in August 1991 from a brain tumour. I spoke to him on the phone just as they were coming round to shave his head for the operation from which he never recovered. He was far too young to have left us.

The goals really started to flow for me in November and December. In fact, I scored four times on the trot. In the League Cup at Anfield we were winning 1–0 for most of the game only for Emlyn Hughes to equalise late on. On the evening of the replay the wind was blowing a gale towards the Paxton Road end and the rain was sleeting down, so we were lucky to win the toss to kick that way. They did not know what hit them as we scored three goals in 20 minutes. I scored twice, with two piledrivers, John Pratt contributed a third goal and the game finished 3–1.

Liverpool, of course, were a great side then. I played in some great games against them but we never won at Anfield: it was our jinx ground. In fact Spurs hadn't won there since 1912 when the *Titanic* went down. In one game we were 2–0 up at half time only to lose 3–2. In another, Pat Jennings saved two penalties, receiving a standing ovation from the Kop, but we still only got a draw. On that occasion Tommy Smith and Kevin Keegan had a barney as to who would take the first penalty. Keegan ignored his captain and placed the ball on the spot only for Pat to make a good save. Smith took command for the second one, only for Pat to make an even better save. It was the only time I ever saw Pat show any emotion on the football field, clenching his fist at us with delight.

Many of our games against Liverpool seemed to

be at 11 o'clock on the morning of the Grand National. One time we stayed at the Holiday Inn, which is near the station. This was in the days of the IRA and the Troubles in Northern Ireland, and at about two in the morning there was a bomb scare. The hotel phoned all the rooms and said, "We have had a warning; everybody needs to gather in the car park downstairs." We all grabbed a shirt and trousers and rushed down to the car park. Phil Beal was in a room with Mike England. He woke Mike up and Mike started getting dressed. But Mike didn't rush. He started combing his hair, putting a tie on, spending all the time in the world getting ready. Bealy is going, "For fuck's sake Mike, get a move on." Mike is saying, "Just a minute." When he came out of the room Mike went to the lift, pressed the button and waited for the lift to come up. Bealy is going, "What are you doing? We have to get to the car park; there might be a bomb in the hotel." But that was Mike for you. He was so laid back off the pitch.

We got my lucky team Wolves in the semi-final of the League Cup. We beat them 2–1 away and drew 2–2 at home with me scoring the deciding goal. For the third year running we were in a cup final. Wembley was becoming the club's second home and Spurs had never been beaten there. Our opponents were Norwich. The final was a very dour game with Duncan Forbes, their physical centre half, trying to nullify me.

John Pratt pulled his groin in the first ten minutes

and Ralph Coates came on to replace him. Late in the game I took a long throw-in, aiming for Alan Gilzean at the near post. The ball was partially cleared to the edge of the penalty area and Ralph belted it into the bottom left-hand corner of the net. His hair went mad as he went on his famous run round Wembley. The pitch was much too heavy and we were too knackered to follow him so we just waited for him to calm down and come back to us. Stevie Perryman was the only one with the energy to catch him up and congratulate him. At the end of the game Bill was very non-committal. More than anything I think he was just very relieved that the Spurs record of never being beaten in a cup final was still intact.

Once again, after the official reception we all bombed off to Morris Keston's party at the Hilton to party the night away. All our families were there plus friends of Morris and other footballers like George Graham, Terry Venables, Frank McLintock, Bobby Moore. They were all good friends with Morris. He knew them all. They all used to go to the Anglo-American boxing club at the Hilton and meet up there. Boxing evenings were quite popular in those days so it wasn't strange to see other footballers at these parties. Stan Flashman, the famous ticket tout, used to invite me to loads of parties, including Arsenal ones. That is how I built up a friendship with Peter Storey.

In the UEFA Cup, we beat Lyn Oslo, Olympiakos and then we came up against Red Star Belgrade. Eddie

Baily had been to have a look at them and came back raving about how they were the best team he had seen for a long time. They, apparently, were big and strong with skilful strikers and two overlapping full backs, which was unusual for a continental side. We beat them 2–0 at home, which gave us a fair cushion for the away tie. The stadium in Belgrade was bursting at the seams with 75,000 inside. We absorbed the pressure for three quarters of the game during which time their star international Dragan Dzajic – nicknamed 'the Dragon' – ran Joe Kinnear ragged, turning him inside out, delivering dangerous crosses that tested our defence to the maximum. Their centre forward eventually got on to one of his crosses leaving us five minutes to hang on by our teeth. We managed it. Exhausted but victorious we staggered to our dressing room and flopped onto the benches, for Joe to appear making an enormous effort to look into an imaginary pocket in his shorts, shouting "Dzajic, are you in there?" It was typical of the way Joe would cover any embarrassment. We could only laugh our heads off knowing he had had the roasting of his life by Dragon. The one thing that Joe Kinnear did not lack was confidence: he had it in abundance both on and off the field.

In the fourth round we played the Portuguese side Victoria Setubal. It was one of the nicer, more civilised trips of our European campaign. Setabul was a fishing village just south of Lisbon. The night before the game Phil Beal chose Dover sole from the menu but he had to take a phone call just as his plate arrived. On his return he found a silver dish considerately placed over his meal to keep it warm. On lifting it, all he found on his plate was an enormous fish bone and head. There was lot of sniggering going on around the table, especially from Cyril and Pat. But there is one person on this planet you do not play a trick on and that is Phil Beal, who is the master of all jokers. The following morning Phil went to the fish market and asked the men for some fish heads which he was happily given. He then sneaked into Cyril's room and put them into the bottom pillow case on his bed.

After the game Cyril kept saying to Pat, his roommate, "There's a hell of a smell in here." He slept on those mackerel heads all night and was asked by the players in the morning if he had noticed any smell in the room. "Funny you should say that . . ." he said. Never take the piss out of Phil Beal. The first place that he looked for on any away trip was the local joke shop and he would buy plastic dog poo, fart and sneezing powder and laughing bags, which drove Eddie Baily crazy. Phil was the unsung hero of Spurs who undoubtedly would have won full honours for England were it not for the great Bobby Moore. His name was pencilled in on the team sheet every week without fail by Bill Nicholson as long as he was fit enough to drag himself off the treatment table, which he seemed to own for four days of the week. A quick few sprints on a Friday morning and an acknowledgement from Phil would confirm that he was ready for the game the next day.

Anyway, we arrived in Portugal 1–0 up from the first leg after Ray Evans had scored from one of my long throws but in the return game Jose Torres, the six-foot-five Portuguese international centre forward, gave Mike England a torrid time. It was a completely one-sided game and we found ourselves deservedly 1–0 down at half time. I got the usual bollocking but this time I really was having a bad game. We were 2–0 down heading into the last ten minutes but we got a rare free kick outside their box. I normally took free kicks from central positions and stood over the ball about 20 yards from the goal. I pushed everyone away and said, "Just let me have a shot." I hit the ball as hard as I could and it was like Moses parting the Red Sea – the wall disintegrated and the ball flew into the top of the net. It was the first and only time we had won by the away-goal rule.

We did not deserve to win but like I said earlier – that's football. On the coach back to the airport everyone knew I had not played that well and Joe and Cyril started their wind-up game, directed at Bill Nick this time, who was sitting just in front of me. They shouted, "Well Chiv, we can see tomorrow's headlines now – *Chivers Saves Spurs Again! Chivers Magnificent! If It Hadn't Been for Chivers Spurs Would Have Lost!*"

All the time they were shouting this I could see the steam coming out of Bill's ears. Finally he stood up, turned around and snapped, "Not if I've got anything to do with it. I'll let the press know how he played: he had a bad game and that goal was the only bloody thing he did."

In football, a striker always gets a chance to redeem himself by scoring a goal, even if he isn't playing well. I could play like a drain for 89 minutes and make up for it with one shot. A goalkeeper can't do that. He can play brilliantly for 89 minutes, make one mistake and be vilified all week. It was lucky I loved scoring goals so much.

My long throws had now become a feature of our play and I practised them in training until my shoulders ached. We had two ways of attacking the goal with my throw. The first was for me to pin it on the glossy head of Alan Gilzean at the near post and for him to flick it on to Martin Peters coming in from behind. The second involved waiting for Mike England to run forward to meet the ball at the penalty spot.

A TV programme decided to run a competition at Chelsea to see which footballer could throw the ball the furthest. I threw mine 130 feet but was disqualified because my toe touched the line. I always presumed the distance I got with the ball was because of my very big, wide shoulders. To this day I have difficulty finding suits and shirts to fit me.

We went out of the 1972/73 UEFA Cup to Liverpool in the semi-final. As I've already mentioned, there was never very much between our two sides at the time, with one goal usually all that separated us. On this occasion it was Steve Heighway who popped up with the away goal, putting Liverpool through. Liverpool were the best team in England at that point, definitely the strongest. Shanks was a great manager but even so we always gave them a good game, and we certainly did over those two legs. It might have been near the end of the season but every player on that pitch gave their all.

> *"For both teams to give that sort of display after each playing more than 60 games this season was unbelievable. It was a fantastic game."*
> **Bill Shankly, *The Daily Telegraph*, 26th April 1973**

Unlike these days we had a squad of only 16 players and nearly all of us played every minute, every game, twice a week. This was whether you were 100 per cent or, more likely, only 75 per cent fit. Spurs had had a run in every cup competition that season on top of the usual 42 league games. There was no room for tiredness or exhaustion for Bill Nick. He expected 100 per cent every minute, every game, with no excuses.

I had settled into life in London and at Spurs really well from Southampton, but my wife Carol had not. I now had two wonderful little girls, Andrea and Melanie. Melanie was born at home on 23rd November 1970 but despite her arrival and having a lovely house and financial prosperity, Carol was not happy. I guess I was just a typical footballer and completely wrapped up in my world. All her family and friends were back in Southampton and she had not made any real girlfriends to pass the time with while I was away, which was often. She did not want to attend many of the occasions that the club invited me to, preferring to stay at home. She wouldn't socialise. At the beginning we had some very happy times, especially around the birth of my daughters, but we had also had some tough times. My injury was not an easy time for anyone and my long periods away from home did not help either.

We had begun to grow apart. Carol began to go home to her mother's house in Southampton more frequently. I had been up and down to Southampton trying to get her to come back home with my girls on numerous occasions. I was terrified of losing them. This went on for about a year. I was quietly desperate but did not have anyone to talk to about it, not even my teammates because it was so personal. In an effort to help us, we had even been to see a marriage-guidance counsellor to try to patch things up but that didn't work either. All they do is listen to your problems. They can't find any magical answer.

I did not even tell my mother what I was going through. The only person I tried to talk to – perhaps surprisingly – was Bill Nick. I had no father to turn to and I thought of Bill as solid and reliable. I thought that maybe I could talk to him like a son to a father. I was wrong. Bill did not want to know. He also saw no reason for my personal problems to affect my football and continued with his aggressive manner toward me. In the summer of 1973 I was away in Italy on an England tour when Alf Ramsey quietly informed me that a few days back Carol had been all over the front pages of the English newspapers saying she had left me and gone back to live in Southampton. He had specially asked everyone, the team and reporters, to keep it quiet from me until we got on the plane home. He said, "Be prepared, the newspapers and photographers will be at Lancaster Gate when we get back so get ready for a bit of a welcome." All the players were very sympathetic. Bobby Moore, Alan Ball and Mike Summerbee consoled me, saying it was not a good time to happen while I was away. As we were getting off the coach Alf said, "Bye Martin, keep your chin up and I hope everything works out, and by the way have you seen Peter Storey?" Peter, my roommate, had got off the coach first and was taking great delight out of kicking a couple of photographers down the road.

I divorced Carol in late 1973 and thankfully saw my girls every other weekend to help maintain some stability in their lives. We have remained a very close family with all my children being the best of mates, holidaying together, seeing each other all the time. Now with four grandchildren, Carol and I remain friends and even party together with the children and can look back and be proud of achieving a good divorce – if there is such a thing.

CHAPTER TEN

ENGLAND FOR CHIVERS

On 17th October 1973 England played Poland in a crucial World Cup qualifier. If we lost or drew, we were out of the World Cup. We simply had to win. The pressure was absolutely enormous. Three years after reaching the quarter-finals, and only seven years after winning the World Cup, England, the country that invented the modern game, were on the verge of not qualifying for the greatest football tournament in the world. It was unthinkable. The night before the game I was in my hotel room in Welwyn Garden City trying to sleep. As I attempted to get to sleep, my mind drifted back to the start of my England career.

It all began in 1963 when I received a letter from the FA at Southampton Football Club telling me I had been selected for the under-23s. I couldn't wait to rush home and tell my mum and dad. The game was in Rouen, France, and I roomed with Alan Mullery, who played for Tottenham. Mullers was a great fella, a friend to this day. I thought that stepping up in class to international games would be daunting, but it proved otherwise. In fact, as the quality of the players improved, I got improved service and could show off my skills. In the game we were 2–1 down to France and I got the chance to come on for 20 minutes at the end. Not long after, I got the equalising goal with a header.

At the end of the 1964 season, I was selected to lead a Young England side in a traditional game played at Stamford Bridge. It was a match between up-and-coming young England players and the full England team. We drew 1–1. I was then selected for an under-23s tour. John Harris, who was the manager of Sheffield United, was the team's manager.

We played Hungary, Israel and Turkey. Against Hungary at the famous Nep Stadium in Budapest we drew 0–0. It would have been wonderful to have scored in that incredible stadium and I did hit one just past the post after a 30-yard run but it wasn't to be. I was so impressed with the city and all the architecture and statues at this incredible stadium. The dressing rooms were so large you could have played five–a-side football in them. There was not one bit of cover: it was completely open with a running track around the pitch which made the small crowd feel a very long way away.

My old friend Mike Bailey from Charlton made this

trip, as did Terry Venables of Chelsea. Terry was a tidy footballer: he read the game well and kept possession of the ball but I felt he was so busy with his patterns, triangles and squares that he didn't make any long passes through or over the defence for me to run onto. He was more of a square-ball merchant. During the match I had begun to moan about the service I was getting from him. I was frustrated that he never put the ball through to me where I wanted it. We gave each other some verbals and it was bad enough that Venables went to have a word with John Harris, the tour manager. As Venables was the captain, I wasn't surprised not to be selected for the next game against Israel.

In 1965 I played many games for the under-23s, one of which was against Yugoslavia at the Dell. I was thrilled to play in front of my home crowd and my family for an England team. I had come a long way from the rec down the road, that's for sure. After training on the evening before that game, George Horsefall, the Southampton kit man, showed me a pair of the Yugoslavians' boots that they were planning to wear the next day. The old-fashioned fibre studs with the nails inside had worn down so much that only the metal remained and had been hammered down to form a sharp point. And they intended to play with these lethal weapons. Referees did not check studs in those days. Luckily, I escaped injury and my dream was complete when I scored the winning goal in a 2–1 win.

Shortly after that game I got my back injury, which

kept me out of football for five to six weeks. That definitely contributed to me not being considered for the World Cup Squad of 1966. Up until I got injured some were saying I might have a chance. There was also the fact that I was playing Second Division football. My mate Terry Paine made it but he had become an established player whereas I was just beginning to make my mark. I really did feel I had an outside chance of making the squad because of my prolific goalscoring. It just proves that luck plays an enormous part in football and your success.

I was desperately jealous of those who made the squad as I thought I was in the same class as Geoff Hurst, Martin Peters and Alan Ball who had just progressed from the England under-23 team. They were all First Division footballers. I was 21 years old and what worried me most was that it would be another four years before the next World Cup and anything could happen before then.

I really thought I had missed my opportunity and watched enviously at home as England progressed thanks to the wonderful goals from players such as Bobby Charlton and Geoff Hurst. I greatly admired Geoff Hurst, who scored that famous hat-trick in that incredible final. I applauded him for taking his opportunity and making so much of it.

Although, like many people, I believed Jimmy Greaves was the best goalscorer in the country at that time, I understood why Alf Ramsey kept Hurst in the team. Jimmy was very unfortunate to have had an injury but as England continued winning without him Ramsey was loath to change the system and he was proved right. Although wingers were tried in the early rounds in the form of Terry Paine and Ian Callaghan, Ramsey had the courage to change the formation. His 'Wingless Wonders' went on to win the World Cup. Ramsey had stated on TV and in the papers that England would win and his belief was backed up. You can't ask more from a manager.

I continued to play in the under-23s in 1966/67, and my last game for my country as a Southampton player was against Italy at Nottingham Forest's ground. Bill Nicholson was watching from the stands as I scored the only goal of the game, and I'm led to believe that that goal formed part of his decision to sign me for Spurs.

After the end of my first season with Spurs the club went on a tour of Greece but myself and Alan Mullery had to come back early to fulfil our respective international duties. Bill Nick returned with us as he was managing the under-23 tour of Italy, Hungary and Germany of which I was part. It was one of the craziest tours I had ever been on and mainly because of a big character called Alan Birchenall. After the game against Italy in Trieste, we caught an overnight train bound for Budapest. The journey lasted 16 hours on hard wooden seats, an inconvenience we made up for by drinking copious amounts of alcohol. The passport police boarded the train as we entered Hungary but had terrible trouble identifying the players from their passport photos because of the state of their faces with bags under their eyes and terrible hangovers.

The following evening, Alan Birchenall discovered the perfect place to display his talents in the nightclub under the hotel we were staying in. In fact, a handful of the players decided to take over the stage and the microphone to entertain everybody. Because of the bright lights, you couldn't see the crowd from the stage and as the evening progressed a number of players left, leaving Alan all alone in the spotlight.

I could not believe his confidence or his singing voice. After a few great renditions of Beatles classics, the house lights went up to reveal the whole of the FA Committee sitting in the audience. The other players had all sneaked away to bed. The next day Bill Nick gave his team selection for the game against Hungary and worked his way through. "Number 9, Martin Chivers, and it's about time you proved to me that I was right in spending a record fee of £125,000 for you. Number 10, Alan Birchenall and I still think £100,000 is far too much for a cabaret artist." We drew that game and went on to beat Germany 1–0 with Alan scoring.

After winning the League Cup against Aston Villa, all the Spurs fans were beginning to chant "Chivers for England." This carried on for some time. On 30th January 1971 we played Everton. We came out and all the Spurs fans were singing "Chivers for England" but

I had no idea that Sir Alf Ramsey was watching. No one told me.

Everton always gave us a terrific game. They had a very good midfield of Colin Harvey, Howard Kendall and Alan Ball with Joe Royle up front. As usual, the pitch was very heavy and after a couple of chances went begging, we got a free kick inside our half. It wasn't out wide, it was quite a straightforward free kick. I had begun to build up a relationship with Martin Peters now with free kicks and sure enough when Martin kicked the ball I span, just got my shoulder in front of my defender, got my head to the ball and guided it over the top of Everton goalkeeper Gordon West to open the scoring. I also managed to make quite a few nice lay-offs for my teammates in that game. It is something I always prided myself on, that I could make those sort of passes very well. They had chances but Pat was in sparkling form and we ran out 2–1 winners.

After the game there came a big surprise. Bill Nick invited me to go up to the boardroom. I had never been there before so I was very intrigued as to why he had invited me up there. I showered, dressed and then climbed the stairs. When I entered the boardroom, who should be sitting there but the England manager, Sir Alf Ramsey. Bill introduced me to Alf saying, "Alf would like a few words with you, Martin."

Ramsey now turned to me. "Congratulations, Martin. That was a fine game today," he told me. "Your manager has been telling me about your progress and that terrible injury. He has been knocked out by the amount of work that you have put in. You have even surpassed the effort of Dave Mackay when he got his two broken legs. Bill is so proud of you." I could not believe what I was hearing. Ramsey was telling me something that Bill was unable to tell me himself. To cap it all, the England manager informed me that he wanted me to play for England in the European Championships against Malta. I had been selected for my first senior England squad and was thrilled to bits.

I roomed with Roy McFarland, the Derby centre half. It was his first game as well. He had been a tough opponent when I had played against him at Derby. Roy was a classy quick solid defender who was complemented by his sidekick Colin Todd. They were probably two of the strongest centre-backs in the country. I also had two Spurs teammates in the squad – Martin Peters and Alan Mullery.

I was selected for the team, but it was to be an unexpectedly tough introduction to the international scene. The pitch in the Malta national stadium was a great leveller – there was not a blade of grass on the ground and so the ball bounced as high as a house. It was like playing on concrete. We won 1–0 with Martin Peters scoring. But to wear that full England shirt for the first time was such an honour: it's what all young footballers dream of. It was the highlight of my career thus far even though the game had not taken place in the greatest stadium or against the greatest team. However, I must have shown enough promise for Sir Alf to select me for the next game, the European Nations qualifier against Greece.

This would be my Wembley debut for England, 21st April 1971. When we arrived at Wembley on the coach there were a sea of England supporters outside, an incredible sight. I soon realised that this was not the same as when you play a cup final with your team, where half the crowd are your fans. With England at Wembley you are talking about 95 per cent of the people in that stadium cheering for you. I had been in the dressing rooms before my league cup final appearances with Spurs, but we had always been in the away one. This time, I entered the home dressing room. Needless to say I was as nervous as a kitten, especially after we had changed and were waiting in the tunnel to come onto the pitch. Then we were given the order to move forward and that incredible walk into the stadium is the most memorable in my football career. The noise level is incredible, it is a din, an incredible din. When you are playing in such a noise you really feel like you have achieved your dream.

The hardest thing to do was stand still when they played the national anthem. It takes four or five minutes and all you want to do is get on with the game. The adrenaline is pumping, you can't stand still, you are rubbing your hands together, taking deep breaths and just hoping you can make it memorable because there is nothing worse than going out to play for your country and not doing yourself justice. Thankfully, in the 22nd minute I made my mark.

I received the ball just inside the penalty area, went past my marker and drove a low ball into the far corner with my left foot. We won 3–0 and I had scored on my home debut. Afterwards I was absolutely thrilled. You feel so satisfied. You feel as if you have touched the top of your football career. What more can you do except win the World Cup? And with the team we had that was not a bad bet. We played Malta again after Greece, and I scored two more goals.

Next up were the 1971 home internationals. Back in those days these mini-tournaments featuring England, Scotland, Wales and Northern Ireland were played at the end of every season in front of full houses. The fans loved those games against the old enemies that lived north of the border, down the M4 or over the Irish Sea.

The first time I played in the Home Internationals was against Northern Ireland in the match where George Best famously kicked the ball out of Gordon Banks's hands as he was about to release it. This was deemed ungentlemanly conduct by the referee but he did it again the following season against Spurs and he got away with it. We drew 0–0 with Wales and then we faced Scotland, our fiercest rivals, who I always seemed to play well against. In fact, I never lost against them. Our first goal came from a corner taken by Alan

Ball which I flicked on at the near post for Martin Peters to come in behind and score. Then, I got two very good goals, the first with my left foot from just outside the box, the second with a deft lob that looped over the goalkeeper and bounced in.

We then won 3–2 against Switzerland in Basle and 2–0 against Greece in Athens and I scored on both occasions.

The next round of the European Nations Cup saw us facing our sternest test against West Germany at Wembley and in Berlin. At Wembley, up front Gunter Netzer had his best game ever for his country and he and Gerd Muller ran us ragged. They gave Bobby Moore a torrid time. In fact it was the first time I saw the great man flap, making mistakes to the point where he gave a penalty away. Germany deservedly went through, even though we played the better football in the second leg in Berlin.

The following season, before the home international game against Scotland at Hampden Park, Alan Ball and Billy Bremner made regular statements in the papers about what they were going to do to each other when they met on the pitch. According to Bremner, Scotland were going to take revenge on England for the humiliation that had been inflicted upon them the year before. 'Ballie' had goaded the Scottish fans too and answered their 'wanker' signs as we arrived on the stadium with two fingers. He was such a fiery little redhead – he matched Bremner in that way.

As we stood for the national anthems the sound of the bagpipes for theirs made the hairs stand up on the back of your neck. I can understand how the English armies in the wars against the marauding Scots were terrified of that sound as they swept across the Highlands into battle. I was thinking at this point that I was going to get the shit kicked out of me and could only pray that Norman Hunter and Peter Storey were not going to be intimidated and would sort them out. I was up against Billy McNeill, a towering centre half for Celtic, but thank God he was not a dirty player as such. Even so, I could not help thinking that all hell was going to break loose.

In my experience it was typical of the little ones to do all the mouthing off before the game but it took the bigger ones to settle the scores. After the first 15 minutes of battle we hardly saw Ballie and Bremner except for when Ballie popped up to score the only goal. The whole game was fiercely competitive and you certainly had to be aware of defenders coming through you from behind. Because of the game's reputation as a battle, the referee tended to allow a lot of tackles to go by the way, almost as if there were simply to be expected.

After all this Scotland, in their wisdom, decided to celebrate their centenary by hosting a fixture against England. Scotland was cold at the best of times but it was absolutely freezing up there in February of 1973. With all the snow and ice around we thought the game might be called off. However, the Scots had put down straw on the pitch to protect it so it went ahead. We played some of our best football that evening with all the attacking players scoring a goal apiece in a 5–0 victory. My goal was straightforward enough, a cross from the right-hand side which I side-footed into the goal with my right foot. They are the ones you love to meet, balls played six or ten yards from goal. It wasn't a spectacular goal: you just make sure it goes in the net. They all count. The Scots had been routed in their own centenary celebrations. This game is where the idea of the three C's started. The three C's were me, Allan Clarke and Mick Channon – we all got a goal in that game – and the press continued using that name until the dreaded Poland game.

In the Home Internationals of 1973, we played Northern Ireland at Everton's ground because of the Troubles in Belfast. Martin O'Neill to this day states that we won the game in the tunnel that day. As we all lined up to come out, the little Irish team stood there. Martin tells me that next to him stood this towering golden giant glistening with oils like a Greek God. He said he could have licked me all over, and that they went 1–0 down at that moment in the tunnel. He tells me that every time I see him. After all, the Irish are not renowned for having a suntan, are they? I scored both goals in the 2–1 win. Terry Neill was marking me and perhaps remembered that game when he became my manager at Spurs. We also beat Scotland and Wales to win the Home Championship.

By now I was becoming very accustomed to the routine for England home games. It was all quite simple. If there was a game on the Wednesday, we'd gather on the Monday at the Hendon Hall Hotel in north London. This is where England had stayed in 1966 when they won the World Cup, so perhaps Alf was superstitious and wanted to maintain this tradition. Training was done at the Bank of England sports ground at Roehampton, which was quite a distance. However, it was well worth the journey because the pitches were immaculate.

After a breakfast of tea and toast at 8:30 in the morning, we would board the coach wearing our England tracksuits. We would drive to Roehampton and stay there until late afternoon. Training was in the morning and after lunch we were allowed free time to do whatever we wanted. Some would go and play pitch and putt, others would read but basically everybody would relax.

One day Alf asked me if I ever went to sleep during the day and when I said no, he persuaded me to try one of these lovely big armchairs they had in the clubhouse. I did and within minutes I was snoring like a baby. During these get-togethers you could not help noticing the cliques. The Liverpool boys would go off together, and it was the same with the Leeds players but the London players like me were happy to mix in together.

On the way back to the hotel, Alf would randomly designate three players from the squad to decide what the group would do that evening. Normally it would be to go to the cinema, the whole squad forming a long row at the local flicks, or occasionally we would go to see a show. The best decision was to go and see an early matinee of Tommy Cooper at the London Palladium. The theatre was half-full but we made up for that with the noise and laughter we made. He played up to us knowing we were there and it was bloody hilarious, just what we needed before a serious football match.

On these trips and games I grew to like Sir Alf an awful lot. The wonderful and new experience for me was that he talked to players individually. He certainly put me at ease. He just said, "You're here because you're playing well for your club and I want you to play exactly like you do at Tottenham." He never asked me to play out of position. He didn't complicate things.

With the press Alf would hold court and dictate his terms. He'd say, "I will give you half an hour after the training sessions and that's it." The press had enormous respect for him but knew not to expect him to talk publically about players individually which was frustrating for them.

Alf kept you on your toes and your place in the squad could never be taken for granted. After a game, Geoff Hurst said to Ramsey, "See you next time Alf." Sir Alf replied, "If you're picked, that is." Geoff should have said, "Hope to see you next time." You were never sure if you'd satisfied his demands and done enough for him; therefore you were always on your toes with the England team.

I remember playing a bad game for England and thinking, "Oh no, I'll be lucky if I'm in the squad next time," and that's how it should be. If you were selected again you would try and make up for it the next time. You would go out and give it your all because to play for England was the pinnacle. I was always striving to be the number one striker in the country. But I could never relax when I had players like Allan Clarke, Mike Channon, Peter Osgood, Joe Royle, Malcolm MacDonald and Kevin Keegan on the bench or competing for my place.

The draw for qualifying for the 1974 World Cup in Munich put us in a small group of three teams; England, Wales and Poland. In our first match we beat Wales in Cardiff but we slipped up in the return game at Wembley, only managing a draw. Then we travelled to Poland in June to play in the mining town of Chorzow. Poland were an unknown quantity at that time and they caught us on the hop. Bobby Moore, in particular, had a tough time. He got caught in possession and Lubanski scored.

It was a tinderbox of a game with all the pressure on us and few chances coming our way. Sure enough in the second half Alan Ball got frustrated and kicked someone and was sent off. Lubanski then rounded off a good game for the Poles by scoring again late in the second half.

On this trip we also played two friendlies against Italy and Russia. Moscow was sweltering in 95-degree heat but we regained some confidence after our poor performance against Poland by beating them 2–1 in the Olympic Stadium. I got a bad clattering from the goalkeeper as I latched onto a through ball but it never hurts quite as much when you score.

Afterwards I made the mistake of drinking an ice-cold bottle of orange juice – not a good idea after playing in such heat – and boy did I get some stomach ache. I was getting agonising cramps on the coach going back to the hotel where we were due to have a reception. Having got changed into my smart suit, I went down to the impressive dining room and found myself sitting next to Alf Ramsey who noticed the pain on my face. "Are you all right Martin?" he enquired. "My fault Alf, I drank a cold drink, got cramps and Martin Peters says I should try his remedy of a brandy and port." "Well, jolly well have one," he said in his posh voice and ordered me one. I polished it off and felt a little better straight away.

All the players then went on to the British embassy, which happened to be the only place you could get a drink in Moscow. It was not far from the Kremlin, just across the river, and as I arrived, lo and behold, there was a very large tumbler of brandy and port waiting for me. My stomach cramps disappeared completely to be replaced by the most terrible headache. I was completely legless thanks to Alf.

However, I was not so drunk that I didn't notice that my roommate Peter Storey was not around when I got back to my room. Spurs fans would not believe how friendly Peter and myself had become. Despite the fact that he played for Arsenal, we were real mates. But he was a Jekyll-and-Hyde character who would have kicked his own grandmother on the football field. His concentration in watching the ball was noted by Alf, who pointed it out admiringly to me during one training session. All the tough Liverpool and Leeds players asked me what he was like as a person because they found him unapproachable. I never experienced that side of him at all. I told them that I found him to be okay even if he did play for Arsenal and had a habit of kicking me all over the field when we played against each other.

Anyway, Peter finally got back into the hotel room at 4am, just a couple of hours before we were due to leave. I was hanging over the side of the bed without my teeth in, not a pretty sight at any time, when he stumbled in with a story to make most people shudder but too private to relate. He came back with no watch or money on him from the other side of the city.

At the airport Alf enquired of me, "Are you all right. You look dreadful." In those days we had a private chartered BA Trident and I was invited to go up to the cockpit to land at Turin because of my fear of flying. I found myself less frightened because I could see that everything was under control and could see that we were safe, something I have to do to this day by grabbing a window seat. Queuing up at Passport Control, Alf commented that I looked a whole lot better.

Before the Poland game we beat Austria in a friendly 7–0 with practically everybody scoring. Alf had decided to go with Roy McFarland and Norman Hunter in the middle of our defence. This meant that Bobby Moore was dropped, having broken the England caps record in Italy. Bobby was one of the most elegant players I ever played with or against. Who can forget his two greatest moments, lifting the World Cup and playing the best game of his life against Pelé in 1970? Bobby played 90 minutes of every game for his record of 108 caps, which cannot be said of some claiming to have beaten it.

Leeds were a group of assassins and Norman 'Bites Yer Legs' Hunter was a major reason for their reputation. Many a time he would pick me up off of the ground after a vicious tackle from behind. Nobody realised that he was pinching me hard under the arms as he picked me up. I would shrug him away only to have the referee's finger waving at me indicating for me to behave myself, just one of Norman's tricks which bloody well hurt. Apart from all this physical play he was a very skilful, talented defender and actually one of the nicest people you could ever wish to meet.

We went into the Poland game full of confidence after that Austrian rout. We knew we were good enough to get a result. Unfortunately Alf changed hotels for the first time from our usual Hendon Hall Hotel and we stayed at a hotel in Welwyn Garden City. But we had been buzzing in training and I am sure that all the players felt the same as me, thinking we were good enough to go out there and beat them. All the pundits on TV and in the newspapers were positive. From the very first minute we attacked them, creating half chances straight away. The ball never came out of their half and I can't remember our goalkeeper Peter Shilton having to touch the ball in the first half an hour. The onslaught continued for the whole of the first half, with the ball hitting the post, being blocked on the line, hitting the goalkeeper, hitting defenders, as well as some other near misses. We were so superior on the night and I just thought that we were going to score any minute. We were not panicking at half time: we just needed one goal and then the rest would follow.

Poland had put all eleven men behind the ball and the only way they were going to score was on a counterattack. Alf was his usual confident self and knew that he could not ask for any more effort than had been shown in the first half. I had a couple of half chances but that is all because there were so many defenders in front of me. The only hope was to strike the ball at goal and hope for the best but it always seemed to get blocked, hit the goalkeeper or hit the woodwork. It was scramble after scramble rather than clear-cut chances. We wanted one goal and I am sure if we could have got it, we would have got three or four. We just had to break that ice and we couldn't do it.

In the second half we pushed and pushed into their penalty area, threatening to score practically every time. Yet that ball simply would not go into the net. We were beginning to get a bit desperate and frustrated as time went on and started to snatch at the ball. We could not believe how well their goalkeeper Tomazewski was playing, out of his skin. The guy, who Brian Clough described as a clown, did not make one mistake.

We had easily had enough chances to wrap the game up but now those chances were beginning to dry up. With the clock ticking, panic started to set in. Channon, Clarke, Bell, Curry and myself all had half chances but not one of us could break the stalemate. I was up against the mighty blond Gorgon who was as big as me and as solid as a rock that day. He was a tough opponent and I did not get a lot of change out of him. I had one or two half chances and that was it. But Alf must have been satisfied with the efforts of his front strikers, otherwise he would have made changes sometime in the second half.

Then, in the second half, out of the blue they broke with the ball on the left wing. Norman Hunter went to put it out of play with his right foot, which was an everyday task for him, but on this occasion he somehow missed the ball and the Polish player stole it and took it on into our half. Because we had been constantly on the attack, we were left light at the back and the ball was squared across to the right-winger 30 yards from our goal. He ran forward and hit it with his right foot. It was a shot that Shilton would normally have easily stopped but incredibly it squeezed underneath his body and skidded into the net off the wet surface. This was the first time he had been brought into the action, having been practically a spectator for all the game.

I immediately thought, "Christ, we have to score two goals now and we haven't been able to score one." Plus the team was tiring: the legs were going with all the effort we had put in. Now they were one up and what the hell were we going to do with 15 minutes to go? But still we created chances, keeping the pressure up. Martin Peters was fouled in their area and we were awarded a penalty, which Clarkey took. How he took and scored a penalty under that pressure was amazing. If it had been me I would have blasted it – that is how I took penalties – but he placed it with such coolness. Sir Alf must have felt that something was going to happen because if we had been having a bad game he would have changed us earlier, but he didn't until right at the end when Kevin Hector came on for me with two minutes to go and even in that short time, he had a glorious chance to score close to their goal line but it was not to be.

When the full-time whistle went there was understandable jeering from the England fans. We had let them down. It was the biggest nightmare of my football career. Losing that game hurt me more than anything else I have ever experienced in football. In the dressing room, all the players were devastated and in tears. Emlyn Hughes in particular had tears streaming down his face. I had never seen grown footballers sobbing their eyes out before. It was desperate in there. Nobody could talk; nobody could say a word to console each other; we were just devastated. We sat there in disbelief.

I was the top marksman in the country and rightly or wrongly people expected goals. That night I had been unable to deliver and it hurt. I am not one to outwardly show my feelings but believe me nothing made me feel worse that evening than the realisation that England were not going to the World Cup finals. I felt that I had let the fans down but more importantly, that I had failed the team and the manager.

All I ever thought throughout my whole career was that I could score goals. I had been so sure of that fact. Going out of the World Cup and not scoring in that Poland game really forced me to ask myself some very big questions. Had I let the side down? Had I let the country down? Had I played my best? Of course I had but then my best just wasn't good enough that evening and that's how it was. It was just unreal.

I remember sitting in the dressing room and thinking to myself, "I am going to wake up soon and it will all have been a bad dream." To have had a game with so many chances and not one bit of luck was unbelievable. Even the goalkeeper – he had been diving but he wasn't really saving; the ball was simply hitting him and ricocheting off somewhere. He did have a great game and so did his defenders but sometimes you have so much pressure on a goal that it puts too many bodies in front of that goal. There was no space at all in that penalty area. They had ten men back and when you face such a packed defence you have to get round the back of them.

But we didn't have any wingers. It was me, Channon and Clarke up front. I don't remember once getting round the back of them on the flanks. Now it would be easy to criticise Sir Alf for not picking any wingers but remember we won the World Cup without them. Sir Alf relied on the full backs and the midfield to make the crosses but because of the nature of the game people like Emlyn Hughes were charging into the box with the ball because like all of us he was so desperate to score. We created 17 chances in that game, 17. But the final shot either hit bodies or the woodwork. Norman Hunter and Peter Shilton had to shoulder a lot of the blame for their mistakes, as did I for not scoring. But no one person should take the blame for that defeat. Shilton was cold: I don't think he touched the ball in the first half it was so one-sided. I would never criticise Norman Hunter. He was a fantastic player. Normally, he would have put the winger into the stands. It just so happened that they caught us cold. If their goal had come earlier I still think we could have turned it around but it happened with about 15 minutes to go.

I thought then that this would be the end of my England career and I was right. I had blown my chance and never did get the opportunity to make amends. For the next game against Italy I was injured and then Don Revie took over and I was not in his plans at all. That remains the most disappointing aspect of my career, that I never got the second chance to put things right as I had with all my other clubs. I have had to live with that for the rest of my life. I can't tell you how upset I was about that one. I honestly believe that we could have gone on and done something serious in that World Cup. Poland finished third in the finals in West Germany and we could have done even better. It was an incredible squad of players, you couldn't have had a stronger England team. What I would have given to score a goal that night.

After the game I went to the Valbonne Club in Soho with Julia – my future wife – and a couple of friends and I drank myself sober. It was such a late night that we were able to pick up the next day's paper on the way home. I didn't really want to read the headlines but I did and it didn't make pretty reading – England had not qualified. For weeks afterwards every time I stepped onto a football pitch fans abused me. It was never face to face, it was always done from the safety of the crowd. I don't think the fans appreciated how much I and all the other England players were hurting. It is a hurt that has lasted to this day. People told me that Alf Ramsey responded to the papers, who were giving me a lot of the blame, by saying I played as he expected me to do and that it was not to be on the night. He managed one more game before finishing as well.

Someone once asked me how you cope with waking up to the knowledge that the whole country is against you? My reply was simple – you grow a beard. And that is exactly what I did in the summer of 1974 in a vain attempt to deflect attention. I stopped shaving while on holiday in Crete. I had deliberately booked my holidays so that I could avoid watching the World Cup.

One day during the holiday I started having a kick-around on the beach with a young boy who had a ball. It was just a kick-about, nothing else, yet when I got home there was an article in one of the papers saying that a ten-year-old kid had been seen running rings around me on a beach and that I couldn't even keep up with him. Fortunately, the father of that child read the same article and wrote a letter to the editor saying how refreshing it was to meet a famous footballer kind enough to have a kick-around with his son and that of course his son had not run rings around me. It was ridiculous but that was the kind of criticism I had to put up with for several months. I didn't even watch the World Cup finals. Actually, I watched the first game when East Germany beat West Germany but that was it. I couldn't bear to watch.

As for the beard, I kept it for 16 years and finally shaved it off for charity.

Much later on in life I remember I went down to Southampton to do some sessions for the Bobby Moore coaching schools. Sir Alf Ramsey came along as a guest of honour. He sat down in front of the children and told them, "We had a wonderful squad in 1966 when we won the World Cup and even better players in 1970. But you have got Martin Chivers here with you and he was a part of the team that was even stronger in 1973. If they hadn't come unstuck in the Poland game they could have gone on to do something serious in the World Cup. The players we had were in their prime and would only get even stronger."

Dreams do not last for ever but at least mine had come true. I had earned 24 caps for England and scored 13 goals, an achievement of which I am very proud. My blue caps have faded in the cupboard but my memories are as bright as ever.

CHAPTER ELEVEN

WHAT HAVE THEY DONE TO MY GAME?

Back when I was playing, football clubs felt they owned you. They paid you a salary and could do what they wanted with you. Transfers and salaries were so straightforward. Once the maximum wage was abolished in the very early 1960s, players had to negotiate their own contracts. Agents were few and far between. In 1973, I received £200 a week and bonuses were the same for everybody. We received £30 a point. To play a game for England I got £60 and at that time we could be taxed up to 83 per cent at the high rate of tax, which I reached every month. I had no other revenue, no advertising or sponsorships. Luckily, they bought this pensions benefit scheme in which meant that instead of paying some tax I could take out a pension and put the money into that scheme.

At the beginning of the new season in 1973/74 I started negotiating a new contract even though it was not up for renewal until January 1974. When I first joined Spurs I signed a three-year contract and in 1971, I did the same. In those days the norm was to sign for three years with a three-year option so after three years the club could either let you go or offer you exactly the same money as you were on at that time.

But football was starting to become more of a business. We had 50,000 supporters turning out to watch us every week, and we started to feel that if we were the attraction, we should benefit in some way without it all going into the club's coffers. We thought a reasonable solution was to receive a crowd bonus which was a suggestion presented to Bill by Martin Peters, as captain, and Mike England, who was the players' spokesman. Bill Nicholson agreed and he produced an A4 piece of paper for the first-team squad detailing the new bonus structure, which he intended to implement for the forthcoming season as part of our contracts.

On that piece of paper he offered a crowd bonus and a new accumulating win bonus which he assumed we would all accept without question. He saw it as a way of pacifying us by allowing us to earn a little bit extra. The players did not agree and questioned the amount because it was insultingly small. On being informed by Peters and England that the offer was not good enough and unacceptable, Bill fumed and blasted them with abuse. "Right, I understand some of you are not happy with this offer, and if you don't want it, you can sod off. Don't sign it and you can remain on your existing contracts."

He got really nasty. He had never before had a representation from the squad and never been challenged *en masse* by the players. He must have been concerned that we were beginning to think for ourselves and flex our muscles. The worm had turned and he did not like it; what's more he did not know how to cope with it. His attitude was that we should just be proud to be wearing the Spurs shirt without thinking of benefits in monetary terms.

From our point of view, we had started seeing older professionals coming out of the game with absolutely nothing. We knew we would be finished at 35 years of age and we didn't want to do so without some kind of financial security. Wonderful memories do not put food in your children's mouths. Eventually the dispute was settled. For every 1,000 spectators in a crowd of over 35,000 each player was to receive £2. Bill also introduced a very complicated win-bonus system. We already received £30 per point for a win. Now, if we won three games in a row our bonus per point would increase by £10 on the fourth consecutive win. If we lost the fourth game we were back where we started.

On one occasion we actually reached five wins on the trot and came up against Leeds away which at any time was a hell of a tough one. We drew the game and were sent us back to square one, which we all thought was really unfair. We had to grin and bear it because we had all signed our contracts. A draw at Leeds on any day deserved more than that.

Gilly was always late for games but around this time we reckoned he was on the turnstiles counting the people coming in to make sure we were not being diddled. Every time we ran out for a match he would be surveying the stands and terraces. We would ask him, "How many do you think Gilly?" and he'd reply "There's about 45-47,000 here today." We always felt that the official attendance announced by the club was a lot less than the actual crowd. Sometimes it was announced as 40,000 or so, even though the ground was jam-packed and the fans could hardly move on the terraces.

There was no merchandising of any note to make money from in those days, except if you were lucky enough to play at Wembley for your club or England. On those occasions, during the afternoon rest before the game, we would put our football boots outside our hotel room door and the boot fairy would come. She had a white paint brush and would add either three downward stripes or one horizontal stripe depending on which company's fairy got to your boot first. Also snuggled away in the boot would be £200 in crisp new notes. That was three times as much as we were paid to play for England and was very welcome.

Today, players earning six-figure sums by way of sponsorship or advertising is taken for granted. Back then you could only grab a bob or two extra where you could. Once Alan Gilzean and I were asked to open a garage in Hertford. I arrived in my best purple crimplene suit and Alan was dashing in mohair. We cut the ribbon and chatted politely to the invited guests for an hour or so.

We had no idea of how to make proper arrangements for a fee and at the end of the event were presented very ceremoniously with a crate of beer for which we were duly thankful. Over time, I got some help. Jack Turner could not really have been called an agent, more an adviser. He got me on *The Ken Dodd Show* with Trevor Brooking where we made complete prats of ourselves – I ended up on the floor with six girls in leather boots on top of me. That TV appearance did not add a great deal to the Chivers coffers but was certainly not taken for granted. It was treated as a little earner. Unlike the poster advert Jack arranged for me. It was the time of the Green Cross Code Man road-crossing campaign and I starred in a government ad to stop litter. It was titled 'Head for the Bin' and showed me heading a ball into a litter bin. I got nothing for that.

However I did earn two very welcome lots of £2,500 for promoting the Subbuteo game. Today players drive around in Bentleys and Ferraris. I was lucky enough to be sponsored by a Ford garage in Hertford who allowed me to drive their new Ford Zodiac of which I was very proud. It is such a shame they don't make bench seats anymore. All the players got to know lots of the fans who were in business in some way or another and because of them I got furniture and clothes much cheaper than normal. Those were my perks as a footballer.

During this time all the players, especially Mike England, had noticed I was down in the dumps. The end of my eight-year marriage had not been easy. Mike, the socialite, took it upon himself to try to cheer me up by arranging a blind date. I jokingly requested a six-foot blonde with big boobs like the Bunnies in the Playboy Club I had started to frequent. Mike got the order completely wrong. He introduced me to Julia who was the opposite, except the blonde bit. We went to see the film *The Getaway* and then afterwards went onto to a London nightclub called Tramp. We hit it off that evening and married a year later. We had two great sons, Nick and Luke, and we have been together since through thick and thin for 34 years.

Footballers were always popular with the fairer sex and in those days we got a lot of fanmail from girls. I remember one letter as being memorably hot. It said, "I am a regular fan and season-ticket holder. I usually stand on the lower shelf, three rows back. I love when you come over to take a throw in. The way you set your shoulders, your rippling thighs." It went on and on. "You came over the other week and looked right at me." It finally ended, "Best regards, I hope you respond to this letter . . . George." I did not reply to it! On Valentine's Day I got a gorgeous card and saw it was from Frustrated George of Camden Town. I threw it away much to Julia's amusement. She had sent it.

That 1973/74 season, we started our UEFA Cup campaign in Switzerland against Grasshoppers of Zurich. It was the very first time we had ever been given the opportunity of warming up before a game. There was a grass training area adjacent to the ground and Bill Nicholson asked us if we would like to warm up on it. This was the normal practice of all European teams including those in Switzerland. Most of us realised it was a very good idea but one player refused point blank to do it. Phil Beal said, "No way, I am not changing my routine before the game."

Phil always insisted on going out last onto the field. Every player had his superstitions and little routines but I was prepared to try this. To be able to comfortably kick the ball about for 15 minutes and warm-up your legs, testing your boots, the temperature of the air and the feel of the ball, was fantastic. It is now common practice to have this pre-match warm-up. For a country that invented football we had a lot to learn from the continentals. This was one of them and another was how to treat injuries. All English physios recommended hot and cold treatment straight after getting a knock, but the Europeans believed wholeheartedly that ice alone was the answer. How right they were.

Mind you, after the first 30 minutes of the Grasshoppers game we were thinking that perhaps the warm-up had not been such a good idea. Pat Jennings was tested to the full, stopping shots from their exceptionally fast centre forward, who got through on several occasions. It was a very open and free-flowing game with them on the attack most of the time. If it had not been for Pat, who played out of his skin, we would have been three down in the first half. Eventually we won 5–1 but in the dressing room afterwards Bill said, "It might be 5–1 on paper but, to be honest, you all ought to give your bonus to Pat Jennings because he kept you in the game." Although it was the truth, we had come to expect nothing less from Pat. We were just so confident that he was never going to make mistakes as he was so steady and completely unflappable.

Pat had every player's respect and never got any criticism. He was the quiet man with the big hairy hands. He was calm and reliable, a superhero, and his achievements prove how right we were to be so confident in him. He has received every accolade possible in football. One season I had a good chance of being voted Spurs Supporters' Club Player of the Year after scoring 43 goals. No way. They voted for Pat because he was always supreme.

Our first three home games in the league that season produced a Tottenham record – we lost all of them. This had not happened since the 1912/13 season.

After seven games with only two away wins to our name we played Liverpool at Anfield. We were 2–0 up but as ever lost in the dying minutes, not helped by a twice-taken penalty and a soft shot in off the post. We finally picked up points at home in the next game against Derby, before Gilly and I got the goals to beat Arsenal on 13th October. A month later we beat Man United 2–1 at the Lane. I scored one from the edge of the box and then later in the game we were awarded a free kick. If the kick was just outside the box, I normally took them. Suddenly from nowhere behind us, Cyril Knowles popped up and bent the ball around the wall into the bottom corner. I was fuming until it hit the net, when we all jumped on him.

In December 1973 we played a testimonial for Phil Beal against Bayern Munich, which would normally have meant a full house. Poor Phil. First Bayern Munich charged him to come over and play and then there was a power cut, one of the many that winter, resulting in a much lower crowd. He just about broke even on the game. It was very unfortunate for a player who had played for the club for 14 years and genuinely thought the best moment of his career was every time he pulled a Spurs shirt on.

Dinamo Tbilisi was yet another team which Bill Nick raved about as being the best he had seen in Europe. We drew 1–1 with them away in Georgia. During the return match Martin Peters and I perfectly executed a free-kick routine we'd been working on in training. After a defender had fouled me, I would walk with him back towards the far post giving him a lot of verbal abuse, which is an international language. The idea was to take his concentration off the ball. We two Martins had developed a fantastic understanding and were totally aware of each others' movements at all times, particularly on free kicks. I would watch him out of the corner of my eye. He would bend down, touch the ball and step back two paces. That was my signal to turn and sprint for the near post. He'd immediately fire the ball in and I'd be favourite to meet his cross, having left my marker standing. It worked more often than it failed. In that game, I scored two.

This tactic had worked well for Martin at West Ham with Geoff Hurst and I had taken over his role. It was no coincidence that when Martin arrived at the club in 1970 in exchange for Jimmy Greaves, we started to win cups. He was a major influence on my game and always seemed to know where I wanted the ball, whether it was into space or to my feet. Our moves in front of goal were always clinically executed and were the result of many rehearsals on the training ground. In the beginning, Martin found it hard to please the Spurs fans because he had taken the place of an icon in their eyes. But he eventually won them round with his brilliance. He was a class act. He scored many goals from midfield; he was energetic and very skilful, and he could get stuck in. That last ability was not always appreciated by the majority of the fans.

Off the field he was a gentleman, one of the reasons he got the captaincy.

As usual, the team's performances were inconsistent due, I believe, to the demands put upon us. We had a squad of only 16 players and we played every Saturday and Wednesday: it was proving difficult to fully concentrate at 100 per cent in every game, let alone be fully fit. It was a much more physical game then and the tackles and constant body contact took their toll. Yet we were progressing in the UEFA CUP.

As the 1973/74 campaign progressed, Bill kept seeing the "best teams ever" in Europe when he analysed our opponents. Now it was FC Cologne's turn, a team who were unbeaten at home in Europe. We thrashed them 5–1 on aggregate and progressed to the semi-finals against Locomotive Leipzig, who we beat 4–1 on aggregate. Our opponents in the final were the Dutch side Feyernoord.

We always found Dutch teams to be very well organised, especially in defence. In the first game at home we were caught offside on numerous occasions, which was very frustrating for us forwards. Thanks to Mike England and an own goal we scraped a 2–2 draw.

Before the return game in Rotterdam there was not a hint of what was to come. Although it was 2–2 and we were away, once the game started we had just as good a chance as any of winning. Early on, Stevie Perryman hit a chance just wide of the post. It was from a worked free kick. Martin Peters took the kick and they thought he was going to set it up for me. But instead he scooped the ball over the top of the wall and Stevie, who was standing at the end of that wall, span round, hit it with his right foot and it just went past the post. Could have been a great goal. Then we had a goal controversially disallowed. Gilly didn't play in this final and it was his replacement Chris McGrath who scored and we couldn't work out why it was disallowed. To this day I still don't know why the ref didn't give it. Then Feyernoord scored and I don't know if it was the disappointment of that or of seeing us going so close or something we were unaware of in the crowd, but suddenly smoke and flames started to engulf one part of the ground. I looked up and saw a person hanging off the stand and behind him seats being thrown into the air like missiles, some of them on fire. It was scary stuff. Fortunately, the half time whistle came so that we could get away from it and regroup together as a team in the dressing room.

However, this was done without Bill Nick who was out on the pitch with a megaphone trying to calm the Spurs supporters and pleading with them to behave themselves. In the dressing room, we were shaken by what had happened and in a bit of a daze. Eddie tried to give us a team talk but all we could hear was the distant noise of firecrackers, shouts and screams.

As I discovered later, the scene was actually getting worse with more glass smashing and seats set on fire.

A lot of the crowd fled their seats including most of the players' girlfriends and wives. They went into the tearoom. However, Julia stayed because she was under a stone shelter and all the bottles were hitting the top of this dugout. She was actually safer in this dugout and was able to watch all the mayhem going on around her. Meanwhile Eddie was trying to give a talk to the team whilst Bill pleaded with the fans to stop rioting and calm down. It was hardly ideal.

We played the second half amidst all this chaos, trying to concentrate on the job at hand. They scored another goal but I don't remember much about the game. We lost 2–0 and after the final whistle Bill looked devastated. He was inconsolable about the behaviour of some of our fans, more so than us losing. He had absolutely no understanding of such behaviour and I remember him looking sadly out of the window of the coach back to our hotel and saying, "What have they done to my game?" It was unusual to have him so quiet and subdued. The fans had let him down but for us it was the knowledge that this was the first time Spurs had lost a final. We just could not wait to get home. All I remember is Bill shaking his head all the time. In the past he had never sought to comfort anyone and so we didn't feel we could comfort him. It wasn't the sort of thing you could do with Bill as he could never sympathise with us. We returned to the hotel in a daze and we all went to bed.

The next morning we had to kill a bit of time before

the flight so we went and visited this new superstore. We were like ghosts walking around that place. No one spoke to each other. There was no smiling, no talking: everyone was deadly serious. Moreover, we felt so sorry for Bill because he took it worse than anybody. Then we got the flight and we went home.

Over the summer of 1974 I was in negotiations for a new contract and had been given a written promise of a testimonial match after I had been at the club ten years. At 29, I still thought I had a future at Spurs and I was still confident that I could score goals. The fact was that Bill would not meet my demands and I refused to sign the contract he offered.

I had already signed two contracts with the club, both of them for three years and on each occasion I had fulfilled all my commitments, I hadn't asked for more money or made any demands throughout either of them. Therefore, if I was going to sign a third I expected an increase in money. I needed the cash because of the divorce I was going through with Carol.

In the subsequent contract negotiations Bill refused my demands. I in turn refused to sign so he placed me on the transfer list. To add insult to injury, at the start of the season, Bill put me in the reserves. Unfortunately the new season started with four straight defeats for the Spurs first team. For Bill, that was it, he'd had enough. On 31st August 1974 he resigned. At the time the press suggested that the argument over my contract was the reason for his leaving. This was not true. In fact Bill wrote in his book that I was not responsible, that his resignation was due to an accumulation of many different things. For example, he was devastated after that Feyenoord game. It really affected him and I think he felt things were slipping away from him.

I know that Martin Peters and Stevie Perryman went to see him and tried to talk him out of leaving. It was a futile task. The game had changed considerably since Bill took over at Spurs in 1958, much of it not to his liking. We had already lost Gilly and certainly some of the remaining players had peaked. In truth, I don't think Bill ever got over the events of that awful night in Rotterdam.

This may come as a shock to Spurs fans but at that point I was not sad to see Bill leave the club. Not as sad as some players, that was for sure. All my time at Spurs, I had been in conflict with the man. Although he and Eddie had undoubtedly made me into a better footballer, it wasn't a marriage made in heaven.

Moreover, at my age I wanted financial security either with Spurs, which was my preference, or if not, by moving on. Bill didn't understand the effect my divorce was having on me both personally and financially. He simply wasn't equipped to deal with such matters, even though they impinged directly upon the club. For me, and I guess for Bill, the time was right for change. At the same time Eddie Baily also resigned.

EDDIE BAILY ON MARTIN

Jimmy Greaves was going, we knew that. Bill Nicholson said to me one day, "We need a new centre forward; what do you know about Martin Chivers at Southampton? I said, "I don't know anything about him. Who is he?"

Bill told me he had got into the England under-23 team and we should have a look at him. I went to see him in a couple of under-23 games – I think one was against Yugoslavia when he scored two goals – and I reported back to Bill. I said, "He is a lazy bastard. He's a big man but he won't hurt anyone or upset anyone. But he has got one thing – he has a very short backlift and is also beautifully built physically. "But if I am looking at Martin Chivers to replace Jimmy Greaves, then no way. On the one hand you have got a quick man in front of goal [Greaves] *against a big lazy sod who won't move and won't head the ball. I have not seen him once go up, knock a centre half out of the way and head a ball. But he has got this backlift."*

Bill said, "What do you reckon?" I said, "I only give him 50 per cent but if he comes here then maybe we can do something. But we are going to have to get on his case."

We rang Ted Bates and he was very complimentary about Martin. "He is a good man," he told us, "a family man. Doesn't drink, good player." I said, "I have seen him play and he doesn't run." Ted Bates said, "Don't worry: he can run. And he will score you goals. But he will cost you a lot of money."

We went for him but when he got here nobody liked him. All the players thought he was really aloof. You couldn't get at him. As a footballer he was really moody. Yet he knew his own ability. He gave you the impression he was slow and yet he was the fastest player in the club over 60 yards. We used to do a lot of timing at Tottenham, timing players over a distance. I looked at Chivers and I said, "He has got no chance." Yet he proved over 60 yards that he was the quickest: he was like one of those horses you back and over the last 50 yards he picks up speed and wins.

But he wasn't brought up as a target man. He was brought up a gentleman and as I said he was very aloof. Now in those situations I would grab the player and say, "Come on let's go and have a laugh and a piss-up." But Martin, you couldn't get near him. Bill would take me aside and say, "Have a go at Chivers will you? I can't get through to him."

I remember the game against Nantes, I chucked a towel across the room at him, knocked cutlery all over the place. Martin had come in the dressing room after the game and said, "Poor team Nantes!" and I said something like, "Don't you worry about poor teams the way you lot played today." He said something like, "Who are you talking to?" and that was it. I chucked the towel and it got a bit nasty and then Bill came in and there was a hell of a kerfuffle.

Then Martin had two seasons when he touched gold but my job was still to wind him up. And it worked.

Now some people say you never had a go at Jimmy Greaves in the same way that you did Martin but that's because Danny Blanchflower wouldn't let me. Danny Blanchflower loved Jimmy Greaves and he protected him. He would always say, "I'll deal with him". But Martin – we were always on his case because he needed it.

I remember that Wolverhampton game. It was one-all and he hit a screamer from 40 yards into the back of the net. I'm standing on the touchline and he came over to me and he said, "Go on, how do you like that one?" Then he turned away and ran back to the centre circle. I shouted after him, "Yeah, but I won because you scored." What you have to do with players like Martin is accept what he has got. I would have loved him to have been a dynamite header of the ball. If he could have scored more goals with his head he would have been even better than he was. And one thing I must say about Martin is that he was never a nasty man. He would give you the needle but he was never nasty.

I faulted Martin on many occasions but he proved to everyone that he could put a ball in the back of a net. What he wouldn't do – and what drove us crazy – is take the bayonet into the den. The amount of times I stood on a touchline screaming, "Get those legs moving, get stuck in." What Martin would do is try and get there first which is actually the answer to the game. Martin was always clever like that plus he was also honest to himself which is the most important thing.

Towards the end of Bill's management days there

was a situation that arose between Martin and money and they said that was the reason Bill packed it in. But it wasn't true. Bill kept his cards very close and he would only feed you what was necessary. Certainly, I don't think Bill was a great man-manager. I know Martin talks a lot about Bill never putting his arm around his shoulders but think about this – when did Bill ever put his arms around mine?

CHAPTER TWELVE

END OF AN ERA

Bill recommended Danny Blanchflower or Johnny Giles to the board as his successor but the club did not interview either. Instead, much to everyone's huge surprise, they appointed ex-Arsenal player Terry Neill. He came in with an assistant, Wilf Dixon. Neill took me off the transfer list and we negotiated a successful new contract.

Neill's training methods were nothing like Bill Nick's. He strongly believed in the psychology of the game. His bonding exercises started by taking us out with our girlfriends and wives for an evening at the Savoy Hotel. That was his introduction to us. We'd never done anything like this before but we were all prepared to try to work together.

He was a good talker, Terry, but let's face it he had

hardly been successful at Hull where he came from. Neill began by playing the team he thought was strongest on paper so I went straight back into the first team and began scoring goals. However, results were not going for us and each game was a bit of a struggle. We got two new players in, a striker named John Duncan from Dundee and Alfie Conn. Some reserves – Chris Jones, Neil McNab, Mike Dillon, and Keith Osgood – were introduced into the first team squad. In the past Tottenham had only introduced one or two players at a time – but suddenly in one fell swoop six new faces were asked to get results for Spurs.

I was now taken off the transfer list and having signed a new contract was promised a testimonial at the club after I had fulfilled ten years' service. We had come to a new era in the club and I wanted to be a part of it. I knew that I had a great deal to offer and that I was still capable of scoring goals. At first, things between me and Terry were fine. He even agreed to let me go to South Africa at the end of the season to guest for Durban City for three games. It did not take long for him to renege on that agreement, the first of several changes of mind.

His training methods were very suspect as well. Under Bill we had undergone all kinds of different imaginative exercises. With Terry it was all about running and effort. With Bill and Eddie we used to do a lot of training and coaching with the ball. We didn't do any of that with Terry Neill. It was all fitness and stamina. I hated it. He used to give us these jackets with the pockets filled with sand to weigh you down. We had to run and sprint with them. It was just power running all the time. We hardly did any constructive things with the ball. It is the typical answer for any coach who has got a problem. The first thing coaches think when a team is not playing well is, "Ah, they are not fit enough."

Most of the first-team players remaining at Spurs where not exactly spring chickens but had reached the top of their profession with enormous achievements under their belts and a lot of knowledge of the game. I think Neill found that daunting. He had played against them only recently and he knew that people like Martin Peters and Mike England knew more about the game than he did and that is no exaggeration. Also, he was coming in to manage a team that was a family. To then try and run players like Pat Jennings, Phil Beal, me, Ralph Coates, Martin Peters and Joe Kinnear into the ground was not the answer. Of course, you have to be fit at the top level but it was the way we were playing together that was the problem, not the fitness. Nature had taken its course on that great Spurs team. Most of us had played ten years for Spurs and the family we had built up was coming to an end. Neill should have kept Eddie Baily on but he brought in Wilf Dixon who was okay but nowhere near the mark set by their predecessors.

Yet our problems were nothing compared to what happened to Cyril Knowles. Driving home one night, his six-year-old son, Jonathon, was killed in a freak car accident. A stone was thrown up by a lorry travelling in front of Cyril's car and it flew through the windscreen, hitting and killing him as he sat in the back seat. Jonathon was a very popular boy and used to visit the training ground. We used to joke that because of his size, he would make a perfect jockey. It was such a tragedy. Cyril's boy had died, we had lost our first ever cup final, Bill Nicholson had gone and then we get Terry Neill as manager. It was not a happy camp.

By March we were in a bad situation. We were in the bottom six of the table and that was when Martin Peters marched into Neill's office and told him a few home truths, including the fact that he felt he could do a better job coaching the team. He was immediately slapped on the transfer list and went to Norwich City to play some very good football for many years. I tried to do the same after hearing what Martin had done but Neill would not let me go in case I embarrassed him. QPR were interested in me but he wouldn't even consider it. In fact, QPR had come in for me at the end of Bill's reign but he didn't want to meet their request and swap me for their Stan Bowles. He felt Bowles was too old.

Another massive blow came when Mike England, who had always suffered with his ankles, suddenly announced his retirement. For me Mike was the best centre half of his time and Spurs even to this day have failed to find a better man. The spark had gone.

Everyone was leaving or talking about leaving, like rats from a sinking ship. The team was not playing well and we were slipping down the league. Although I was scoring my fair share of goals, the new system of play did not suit my game.

The service was not as it had been. The team started hitting balls at me from just inside the halfway line instead of from the wings. That means the ball is coming at you from such an acute diagonal that it is impossible to get yourself into a scoring position. You have to get the ball level and then cross it for the forwards to feed off it. Furthermore, John Duncan and I did not form any sort of partnership. I just couldn't work with him. Sometimes that happens. My partnership with Chris Jones, for example, was totally different. He was an unselfish player. But John and I did not click at all. Plus, we were in big trouble and did not have the time to experiment and develop. Don't forget we were a poor team and I think we had been knocked for six by that final with Feyenoord. We were all struggling. Mike England, Joe Kinnear and Cyril Knowles had all seen better days although they were capable of playing good games. Martin Peters had gone to Norwich and was doing extremely well there which proves the point.

We were in a terrible state. Sometimes a new manager comes in and sweeps clean and it works. But it didn't work, plus Neill was on my case a lot. "You are not scoring enough goals; you are not working hard enough," he would say to me, even though all he seemed to be doing was getting the team to kick the ball to me from the back and thinking that was enough. Well, it doesn't work that way. You need support. That first season was probably the worst one under Terry Neill. We were in the bottom most of the time and we never got out of there.

Now, I wanted to do my best for the club. I always did. Plus I had some inducements. I had the promise of a testimonial in a couple of years' time plus the chance to make some serious money in South Africa. Halfway through that season I happened to mention to Neill that Durban had been in touch and had asked if I was still coming in the summer. Neill turned round and said, "No, you can't go. You haven't done it for me so I not doing it for you." This was after promising I could go. I said to him, "Well, to tell you the truth you can stick it up your arse because actually I don't want to go now." Gilly had gone out there to play and he came back after just six months with really bad reports. He hated it and so that made my mind up for me. I just wanted to find out what Neill was like and now I knew.

That said, some players flourished under the new manager's regime. These were the slightly younger, fitter ones. John Pratt came into his own as the engine of the team. He had always been a fringe player and had never held down a regular place. Now was his time. Terry Naylor had taken over from Joe Kinnear at right back and also worked well for Neill. Steve Perryman had become captain when Martin Peters left and he began to impose his personality on the team. Perryman was a very skilled and versatile player, highly determined and Spurs through and through. He became a star player who made over 1,000 appearances in a Spurs shirt, a club record to this day. He went onto win the FA Cup twice under Keith Burkenshaw, who came in as manager after the Neill era. However, while there was a lot of effort on the pitch, the quality of our football was poor, we were negative and going nowhere.

With two games to go of the 1974/75 season Spurs were in the relegation zone. By now Neill had put me in the reserves as he looked to Duncan and Jones to score the goals. It was then I decided that I had had enough. I couldn't stand it. Having been left out by the manager for six consecutive games, I finally snapped and had it out with him at the training ground on the Thursday before a Saturday game with Arsenal. I said, "Why don't you let me go? I'm not happy here, you're not happy with me and you are not playing me."

"There is no one interested in you," he replied.

"Do me a favour," I said, "I know there are people interested. Why don't you put me on the transfer list?"

At the end of the argument Neill ranted, "Right – you are finished, you're washed up: you can go."

At last, he had conceded.

"Thank you very much. That's all I wanted to hear," I said.

I was relieved but suddenly I was faced with the prospect of having to leave Tottenham, my second home, my favourite club, to play for another club. But what choice did I have? None.

Ralph Coates, who was injured, travelled with me on the team coach to Arsenal for the big north London derby, both of us dressed in our civvies. Together in the stands we watched Spurs lose 1–0 and we all climbed back onto the coach for the return journey knowing that Spurs would have to beat the mighty Leeds United at White Hart Lane on Monday evening to stay in the First Division. Terry Neill stood up at the front of the coach and said, "Listen, I want everyone to report to the West Lodge Hotel in Hertfordshire tomorrow night." As we got off the coach I enquired if he meant everyone including me because I had been told I was washed up and could go. "When I said everybody, I meant everybody," he replied. Then he added, "I'll drive past your house at quarter past six and we can go down there together."

On Sunday evening he came past – he only lived around the corner from me – and tooted his horn. I followed him in my car. When we arrived at the hotel he took me into a room and introduced me to someone I'd never seen before. "I'd like you to meet a friend of mine; his name is Romark." Then he said, "Romark is a clairvoyant." Neill went on to explain that Romark had seen next Tuesday morning's headlines in the papers. All this weird talk was making me very uncomfortable but I remained as polite as I could and asked Romark what the headlines had said. "'Chivers

Back with a Goal'," he said, completely straight-faced. "Do you believe all this?" I asked Neill in amazement. "I'm not even playing, am I?"

"I'm 50-50 at the moment and I'll let you know tomorrow morning," Neill told me. "But first I want to introduce Romark to the rest of the players." As I left the room I bumped into all the players who were surprised to see me there so early. I said, "You won't believe what is coming. There's a fella in there called Romark, he's a clairvoyant." Typically one of the players said, "What's the hell is that?" I said, "He's a man who sees the future. He told me he's seen Tuesday morning's headlines." Terry Naylor, sharp as a razor, said, "Did you ask for the racing results at Lingfield?" We all started to giggle, but I said, "You can laugh but you are all going to meet this Romark at dinner, so be ready."

We all sat around this big boardroom table for the meal and an album was passed around with newspaper cuttings about all the things this Romark had done. He had hanged himself and lived. He had escaped from impossible chains and he was also a hypnotist. The quiet sniggers were becoming louder as it was passed around. Then Romark stood up and introduced himself and started talking to individual players. We did not realise at the time that this was his way of selecting his stooges for his performance later.

After dinner he started his party piece. Cyril Knowles was obviously the prime candidate, the one to be taken to the slaughter. He took Cyril up onto the stage. Cyril was obviously quite proud of being specially selected and winked at all of us. He liked being the star attraction. Romark sat him on a chair and began talking quietly to him. He then proceeded to stick these big needles into the back of his hand. Cyril's eyes never left us and he continued to smirk. There was no reaction on his face.

Romark then took the needles out and arranged two chairs so that Cyril's feet were on the seat of one while the other was placed under his head by Pat Jennings, who had joined them on stage. Romark, who was holding Cyril up with his hands, said to Cyril, "Imagine you are a rod of iron." Then our mouths dropped open when Romark took away his hands so Cyril's body wasn't supported any more and got Pat Jennings to slowly sit down on Cyril's tummy. To our amazement he did not collapse in the middle under Pat's weight. What a trick. But what the hell has all this magic got to do with football?

Terry Neill then announced that Romark wanted to see each player, one at a time, before we went to bed. It was obvious that he was going to try to hypnotise each of us. Phil Beal point blank refused. I was so unsure of this whole circus that I phoned Julia and told her all that had been going on. I told her I thought I was going to be hypnotised. She said, "Don't you dare." Although I really did not want to have anything to do with Romark or hypnotism, I have to confess that curiosity got the better of me.

I was one of the first to go in the room. I had no idea of what was going to happen. I did not close my eyes and to this day I cannot say whether I was anything other than awake and conscious listening to what Romark said. He talked quietly saying, "All I want you to do tonight before you go to sleep is to think about your best games for Spurs and especially your goals."

As I came out of the room all the players were clamouring to ask me what had happened. I simply explained that all he required was for each of us to think of our best games and goals before we go to bed tonight. The next player to go in was Ralph and as he got up to leave, Terry Naylor shouted at him, "Bloody hell Ralph, you're going to have trouble. You had better think about that reserve game you had last week."

Ralph reported back to us that he did indeed tell him all about this great game he'd played. "I told him I was playing for Burnley at Leeds. I'm going down the wing, I've beaten the full back twice, and had some amazing crosses. I have had so much of the ball and now I have the ball again and I've gone past two defenders and hit a perfect 30-yard shot that has just been tipped over the bar." Romark asked, "Was that the best game of your life?" and Ralph replied that it was. "This is great," says Romark. "Now tell me what's the score?" Ralph looks up and replies, "We're losing 5–1."

The next morning while we were training at Cheshunt, Terry Neill walked over to me and told me he was going to play me against Leeds. "You've fallen for it, haven't you?" I said. "Okay, if you want me to play, I'll play." Despite everything that he had said or done, of course I was going to jump at the chance. No professional football player would ever turn down the chance of playing and proving himself.

It was simple. Beat Leeds and we stay up – it was a life or death game. We started well and then Cyril scored the first goal, then Alfie Conn scored and we went 2–0 up. Being the flash little bastard he was, Alfie started to take the piss out of the Leeds players by sitting on the ball. This is the last thing you do to Leeds. We were all shouting at him to stop. They immediately turned up their game and Peter Lorimer smacked in a typical goal from the edge of the box. They had been quite happy to drift through the game until Alfie started winding them up.

Minutes later I got the ball just inside the box, turned and stroked it in to make it 3–1. Romark's prediction had come true – only for Alfie to start sitting on the ball despite our pleas for him to stop. Sure enough Lorimer replied with another goal. Thankfully Cyril scored his second goal and we held on till the end of the game. With that win we avoided relegation by the skin of our teeth. The next day's headlines said, 'Chivers Back with a Goal'.

Some people might think that we had discovered the answer to all our troubles and that we should have bought Romark for a record club fee. Personally, I just think it was desperation from the manager and that Leeds were strolling the game with nothing to play for – it was our lucky day. Later on, a rumour began circulating around the dressing room that Romark had been killed by a number 29 bus. He certainly did not see that coming.

How desperate does a manager have to be to call upon the services of a clairvoyant? In hindsight some people might have said it worked but Neill's coaching methods had always been bizarre. Even though he and I had our differences, Bill Nicholson had the total respect of everyone at the club from those in the office to the ground staff, the directors and all the players including myself. In time it became increasingly obvious that Neill did not have the respect of everyone in the club.

The only good thing that happened in that period was my marriage to Julia that May. Clive Bednash was my best man. He used to run the Room At The Top Club in Ilford. He had become a very good friend and graciously offered us the use of his Rolls Royce, which he himself drove on the day. We got married in Epping registry office and then we went for a blessing at a church in Chigwell. Then we walked across the road and had our wedding reception in a hall next to the pub there. None of my teammates were there because the day was for family. We did have a party later on for all the players and our friends at our house in Chigwell.

The 1975/76 season started with a pre-season tour of Germany where Neill proved yet again that fitness was his only answer to football. No skills, no coaching, no tactics: just running until we dropped. The striker I enjoyed playing with the most during this period was young Chris Jones. We worked very well together, supporting one another and bringing each other into the game. John Duncan, having been bought by Neill, was clearly always going to be first-choice striker, so Chris and I rarely had the opportunity to play together. I alternated with him on the bench. Meanwhile, because I thought I was available for transfer, I was waiting for someone to come in for me but it seemed that I was not going anywhere.

I started to think that I might as well stay because in a year and a half I would be due my testimonial. I also thought at the back of my mind that with the results going so badly, Terry Neill might leave before me and I might get a chance under a different manager. I waited and waited for him to get the sack but the board of directors persevered with him.

One day a gorgeous blond with a hairdryer appeared in the dressing room. His name was Don McAllister. As a Terry Neill signing he was treated with due suspicion. However, he soon became a true mucker with us and it was not long before our wives and girlfriends had to wait in the rain outside in the car park for over an hour after the games. We would eventually appear perfectly quaffed having queued and haggled to borrow his hairdryer. In those days, girls and wives were of little consequence to the club, so there was really nowhere for them to wait for us. They could have a seat to watch the game and afterwards they were treated to a cup of stewed tea in the player's tea room, where you could cut the air with a knife because of the cigarette smoke.

In November I was selected to play against QPR. Midway through the game I was running onto a through ball when I felt a piercing pain in my hamstring muscle. I had never pulled my hamstring in my whole career and my God it hurt. I was poleaxed and carried off to the dressing room. One good thing that Terry Neill did was to bring in a very good physio called Mike Varney. Mike came from the army and was a remedial therapist. He knew just what to do and strapped a great big pressure bandage around my thigh.

Tottenham were due to play on Tuesday in a cup game against West Ham and I went into the club on Sunday morning. The removal of the bandage revealed that my leg was completely black. It had been bleeding overnight and the flesh was hanging out at the back. To this day Mike Varney says it was the worst hamstring injury he has ever seen. Unbelievably, Terry Neill asked Doc Curtin, "What are his chances of playing on Tuesday?" Everyone looked at him in amazement for asking such a stupid question but the doc suggested the only thing he could try was the famous cortisone injection and proceeded to stick the needle into the back of my thigh. As he removed the needle, blood spurted all over the place.

Doc Curtin tried everything but they could not stem

the bleeding with any form of plaster. It kept becoming too soggy with blood so in the end they applied pressure and eventually it stuck. I was out for seven weeks.

Once again, we were doing very well in the League Cup and had got to a semi-final against Newcastle. I had been in and out of the team, slowly recovering from the hamstring injury. However, for some reason known only to himself, Neill brought me back for both those games. We failed to reach the final, though, and finished mid-table in the league.

I hated this period of my career at Spurs. I just did not fit in with Neill's team and his methods which included some strange bonding antics. I found it embarrassing when we were asked to put our arms around each other and do the 'hokey, cokey' in the dressing room. I was too old and sedate for all that nonsense and I showed it.

I was surprised then when Neill selected me to go on the club tour at the end of the season. We played nine games in Canada, Fiji, New Zealand and Australia and won them all. In Fiji, the match programme stated that I was six foot ten, I guess because they had only ever seen me play on television where I appeared so big. When we ran out onto the field, three quarters of their team were taller than me and they commenced to tackle us waist high. The stadium was so small that it could not hold the 6-8,000 fans who were hanging from the trees and stands.

Right in the middle of the pitch was a two-metre wide area of wood shavings which covered a concrete cricket strip. I discovered this after jumping to head a ball only to land with my studs on the concrete. I was carried off with a bruised heel and was unable to play three of the nine games. To complete the carnage, the scaffolding which they had erected to form one of the stands collapsed in the middle of the game causing chaos in the crowd and several injuries.

Young Chris Jones was also injured and unable to play for much of this tour. We were therefore together a lot of the time, having treatment and hanging out. On one of these occasions, Neill returned from training to see us together talking and having a drink. He exploded at both of us and pulled Chris into his room for a meeting.

Afterwards, the boy came to Ralph's and my room nearly in tears. Neill had told him that if he ever saw Chris in my company again, he would be out of the team for ever. I was so angry I went straight to Neill's room to confront him.

"Terry, why don't you just get rid of me? Why do you upset the youngsters? Let me go." When he replied that it would all be sorted out on our return, I did not know if he really meant it because of all the other promises he had failed to keep.

Our last game of the tour was against Western Australia in Perth and I scored a hat-trick. I am really glad I did, as it turned out to be the last game I would ever play wearing a Tottenham shirt. About a week after our return, the phone rang at home. It was Neill. "I've got a club interested in you," he said.

Immediately, I thought it was QPR. "Who is it?" I asked. Quietly, he told me it was Servette in Switzerland. I thought, "Hell, is that far enough away for you?" He told me they were coming over the following day to talk to me at the Park Lane Hotel. I went to the meeting and found the club representatives to be true gentlemen. They told me they were very keen for me to go over and see their set-up in Geneva, of which they were very proud.

I agreed to take a look and not long after flew to Geneva. I was very impressed by what I saw. Neill was immediately on the phone demanding to know whether I had signed. I told him I had more than football to consider. My wife was eight months pregnant with our first child and I had two daughters from my first marriage. Suddenly life turned very stressful. Everything came on top of us. I had been forced into a corner by Terry Neill. I had to sell my big house in Chigwell and move to Brookmans Park. I needed money for the divorce and it also made sense to live near Julia's family. Before we could move in we had to live a month in rented accommodation with all our furniture and belongings in storage. Julia was seven months pregnant and I had to find us somewhere new to live. I was even down to do an FA coaching course at Lilleshall. How our marriage got through all this is a testament to the dogged determination of Julia. How she stayed sane throughout this whole period I will never know. My life at that time certainly pushed her to the limit.

I thank God we got through. Terry Neill did not seem to understand these concerns. It was not just a matter of moving to another club, but to another country with another language, another culture and a long way away from family and friends. I told him I would think about it and he threatened, "You haven't got a lot to think about. I'm telling you if you don't sign you will spend the rest of your contract in the reserves."

I put the phone down and repeated the conversation to Julia and she said, "Martin, you don't have a choice. You're going to have to sign." She knew that I wanted to play first-team football and that if I had continued at Spurs with Neill in charge I would have been miserable beyond belief. Neill did not like the fact that the younger players were looking up to me. It was exactly the same reason he sold Martin Peters. The younger ones looked up more to senior players like Martin and I than they did to Terry Neill. I would have been trapped so I signed for Servette.

A week later Terry Neill resigned and went to Arsenal. I went immediately to the chairman's house and asked Mr Wale if he could possibly stop the transfer but he told me it was too late. He informed me that Terry Neill had told him that he knew nothing about the Arsenal job when he resigned from Spurs. I could not believe the chairman's naivety. I asked him, "Did you believe Neill when he told you that?" and he replied that he had no reason not to. What a joke.

Spurs bought me for £125,000 and sold me for

£80,000. They had eight and a half years' service from me and 174 goals. I was really sad to leave Spurs, really sad. But I was determined to prove Neill and all of my critics wrong in Switzerland.

STEVE PERRYMAN ON MARTIN

I signed pro in January 1969 and got into the first team in September 1969. Chivers was in the team before I got there but he had been injured so I started with Jimmy Greaves and Alan Gilzean up front. Then Greaves went and Chivers came back. He was big, powerful, with a great touch; he had everything you wanted but there was one problem – he just wasn't punching his weight. He would always finish second in challenges. He looked a bit timid, a bit frightened; it was just too easy to dispossess him.

Bill Nicholson's style was always to play the ball up front which then goes back to the midfield, and then forwards again. But it always used to break down with Chivers because for whatever reason he just wasn't right. Whether he was having problems in his mind about his fitness or his injury I don't know; all I know is that he was just not pulling his weight. Now in a team there always has to be a scapegoat and he was the scapegoat. No doubt about it. If Gilzean did something wrong it was like, "It can't be him, it must be Chivers."

Also his body language (not a term you would have used back then) was kind of saying, "I know I've made some mistakes but it doesn't matter because I am a very good player." Well you haven't quite delivered on that yet mate. Chivers was sort of an enigma. You knew that the powers that be trusted him enough to buy him and work with him, but nothing was happening. So you couldn't see it coming right; you couldn't see how this huge talent would be sparked up into action. What was going to spark him off?

As I recall this is what happened. At training one day there was a game arranged and Bill Nicholson told Mike England, our centre half, to kick the shit out of him to see what reaction he was going to give. Nicholson was looking for answers. Has this fella got anything inside of him? Because it wasn't apparent that he did.

Well, the answer was yes because Chivers and England ended up scrapping and from that day on all became sweetness and light. He became the best centre forward in Europe – without a doubt. He developed into the most consistent front player in Europe. Chivers was the man. It got to a point where the ball would go to him and you almost didn't back him up because you knew he was going to score. And he did. Which made you right not to back him up but also wrong because if he hits the post and it comes back, where are you? But we had so much confidence in him.

Things cloud up over time and go into one and I am making a judgement on how he was when he became a proper player but for me he was double surly. Basically Chivers was a selfish bastard and you have to be that to be a striker. He was the kind where if we lost 5–4 but he had scored the four goals he would be happy. Now some players would kid you that they were disappointed the team has lost but really they are delighted to have scored the four goals. He never kidded anyone that way. It was very honest of him. There was an honesty about him. His thing was, "I'm the man and at Tottenham you need to have the man." It was Greaves, then it was Chivers. Lately there have been Hoddle and Gascoigne, but in my time it was Chivers. Not that Bill Nicholson thought so.

If you wanted praise, Bill Nicholson was not the man. Bill Nick put special emphasis on centre forwards. I think he thought your front men are the engines of the train and if they ain't doing their stuff the rest can't follow behind it. That's why Bill Nick was always focussing on Chivers. Eddie Baily was even harder on him. Remember a lot of trainers in those days had come through the army training camps, so it was tough stuff. It was their way of pushing him on. That was the regime.

Because Chivers was languid, it did feel like you needed to push him all the time. It wasn't my job. I wasn't team captain but I tell you this, people always ask, "How would Jimmy Greaves get on in today's game?" Or, "How would so and so play?" Well, I think if Martin Chivers had played today he would have been the absolute bollocks. He would have got what he thought he was worth moneywise and he would have been treated with a lot more care, be that with his body or his mind. To a certain degree I think Martin Chivers was a player out of his era – so to do what he did back then at Spurs is an amazing achievement.

CHAPTER THIRTEEN

THE SWISS TIMES

I made a quick trip to Geneva to look at apartments and to meet with the manager, the board and Dr Conte, who was in charge of the medical. It was a tough one. The doctor was young, enthusiastic and renowned for running marathons. It was a total invasion of my body, he tested me everywhere – and I mean *everywhere* – and it left me weak at the knees. He then said, "We are going on a short run."

He found me a pair of trainers, shorts and T-shirt and off we set. Now remember, I am no long-distance runner. From the start he was always ten yards in front, blabbing his mouth off while I was breathing through my backside. I realised we were running up the side of La Seleve, the mountain at the back of Geneva, and if you remember June 1976, it was one of the hottest summers ever. We eventually returned to his practice when he surprisingly declared that I was quite fit and that I had lasted longer than any other footballer he had taken on a run before. High praise indeed.

Still, despite Dr Conte's praise, and even though I was just 30 years old, I was already thinking about my future after I'd hung up my boots. That's where Lilleshall came in. I thought the Full Coaching Badge was highly respected within the football industry. I was to learn later that it meant absolutely nothing and that getting a job in management was a case of who you knew, not what you knew. About 80 of us took the course, mainly professional footballers who, like me, were hoping to stay in the game. I loved it. It was a little like going back to school as far as the theory went, but I respected the knowledge of the instructors and enjoyed the discipline of the organised coaching. In the second week each candidate had to complete three demonstrations of a coaching exercise, with just a day's notice to prepare. We all took part in each demonstration, supporting the candidate by following his directions. I got something way out of my zone when I was told one of my sessions had to cover 'distribution from a goalkeeper'. The other two were quite straightforward and I sailed through the diploma with flying colours.

I returned home in time to take my wife into the local hospital on 30th June, the date for her to be induced as the baby's head had not engaged. In those days, with an epidural and induction, the husband was not allowed to stay, so I left and went to my sister-in-law's, who cracked open the champagne to celebrate the birth of my first son. I returned in the early evening to congratulate Julia and see the squashed-up face of baby Nick in the intensive care unit.

A couple of days later I had to return to Geneva and join my new teammates for pre-season training. The apartment I had chosen was on the seventh floor of a block in Eaux Vives, situated on the side of Lake Geneva with magnificent views of the lake and mountains. It was very civilised, with all the local woman in little Dior outfits and wonderful smells emerging from the restaurants and boulangeries. All the players were given Honda Civic cars with Servette's name emblazoned down the side. Julia had one waiting for her too.

My welcome into the team was so warm. I was introduced to everyone – the players, the manager, the doctor, the money man and all the board of directors. I soon learnt the continental greeting, which I passed on to my children. Each time you met someone, whether once or twice a day, we shook hands and if greeting a lady, a kiss on each cheek was the expected formality.

My wife arrived one month later with our Nick. It was a difficult start with a new baby and no family and friends but after a couple of months we slotted into a reasonable standard of life and certainly felt less stressed than we had in the summer. we both settled into a very civilised life of eating wonderful food, being in a calm, clean city and eventually making some very good friends. The language was not such a real problem as I spoke very good German thanks to my mother, which even the Swiss players understood as their second language, and Julia spoke quite a bit of French. We both improved our respective languages by going to school each week.

Pre-season training took place in the vineyards outside the city and I immediately lost half a stone and got very fit, although I still had that problem with my bruised heel thanks to that Fijian cricket pitch. It was still hurting like hell.

Peter Pazmandy, a Hungarian, was the manager and a very relaxed man. If I needed him I always knew I could find him in a certain coffee bar smoking with his mates and putting the world to rights. We spoke German together but all the team talks were in French. I gradually picked up the football vocabulary and jargon.

Servette were one of the top teams in Switzerland at that time so we were always going to be near the top of the division. The players in the team were Swiss–German, Swiss–Italian, the home grown Swiss–Romande and a couple of French players who came in each day from just across the border. A lot of black-market goods came through that border hidden in the trunks of their cars, especially wine and meat because they were much more expensive in Switzerland.

My debut was in the pre-season Alpine Cup Competition between French and Swiss teams. We played away at Lens and Metz and I scored in both games. But my first home goal was not forthcoming. I only managed to score away from home. Still, it was a good start. One of these early games was in Sion in the valleys between the Alps. I had a moment of reflection as I stood on that pitch and surveyed a chateau on one side and snow-capped mountains on the other, on a balmy evening with the sun setting. It dawned on me that I was being paid for this. I had rarely felt so lucky.

Grasshoppers Zurich versus Servette was the Swiss version of Arsenal versus Spurs. It was the big one with both teams fighting at the top of the league. The Servette fans had been patient with me at the start of the season and were waiting for me to do something special. On the day we played Zurich I gave it to them. The Swiss–German striker, Kudi Müller, who played up front with me, drove a corner onto the penalty spot. I rose and made perfect contact and the ball flew in above the goalie. It was the best header I had ever scored and pictures of the goal were in all the newspapers the next day. There is one particularly good photo still displayed at the club to this day. Better still, I won the fans over with that header.

The football itself was a bit slower than England: slower to build up, not so frantic but technically as good. The most notable difference was that the defenders were as skilful as the attackers. For the big games in Geneva there would be 20,000 spectators crammed into the small stadium, but on average attendances were about 14-15,000.

People often asked me if I was homesick but I was fine when my family was with me and I also had my mum and my two girls out to stay with us. The beauty of playing in such a country was that we got a winter break because the weather was so fierce and the grounds got covered with snow. This was to be my first experience of being able to celebrate Christmas and the New Year properly, without having to prepare for a game on Boxing Day or New Year's Eve.

I returned to England over the holiday season and went to a few games at Tottenham. When Spurs were awarded a throw-in the crowd would start chanting, "Chivers, Chivers". I had not been forgotten and I was absolutely thrilled by the sound. I was disappointed to have left Tottenham but I never harboured ambitions to manage or coach them. I'm glad I didn't because the love affair I still have with them wouldn't be alive today. As Alan Mullery said to me once, "The one sure thing about being a manager is that you know you're going to get the sack one day."

The first season I was with Servette we won the League Cup against Neuchatel Xamax in Lausanne and came second in the league. They had a very strange points system in the Swiss league – they played two halves of the season and at the end of the first half they halved your points total. We were three points clear of Basle. When they halved the points we were only one point clear. Then they would cut the division in half. The bottom six would play each other and battle against relegation, while the top six played each other again for the championship. We finished up at the end of that season dead level with Basle. We had to have a play-off and we lost it 2–1. So we finished up runners-up in the league but I was satisfied with being third highest goalscorer in Switzerland.

We eventually settled into a good social scene. One night we held a big dinner party for my mother and as I looked around I heard Italian, French, German and English being spoken around and across the table. We even had the manager and his wife around to the apartment for dinner. We became good friends, although his eyes did pop out when he saw my drinks trolley. He never objected to a glass of wine even before a game but spirits were another matter.

A lot of the socialising revolved around food. I had met up with a group of ex-pats, most of whom worked at international bodies in the city like the World Health Organization, the United Nations and European Organisation for Nuclear Research (CERN) for whom my future best friend Ray Lewis worked. Ray had approached me to coach some of his workmates for Sunday morning games. The only problem was that when I stood on the line Sunday morning as coaches do, the referee came across and demanded I stop shouting. They believe in silent encouragement in Swiss Sunday morning football. Ray is now godfather to my son Luke and we have spent many happy skiing holidays in Verbier with him since. For the two years I was there, the club never encouraged me to go near the mountains and after trying to learn to ski at 40, I understand why.

One day, Ray took me to his place of work and I was shown around the three kilometre tunnel which they bombard with nuclear particles to try and find out about the Big Bang theory. A physicist friend of his tried to explain all this to me but it went straight over my head. On the news recently I saw that the tunnel had now become about 20 kilometres. The English ex-pat crowd were a rowdy lot compared to the rather more sedate people of Geneva. I remember one particular evening in a classy restaurant with about ten of them. By mid-evening we found ourselves all alone as the other clientele had disappeared. This may have been due to the fact that the whole meal at our table was carried out reliving the film *The Life of Brian*. We had several John Cleeses, Biggus Dickuses, centurions and Brians all delivering lines in very loud voices.

My second season at Servette saw me scoring regularly and in one game against St Gallen I scored four goals and missed a penalty. The league title was once again a ding-dong affair between us and Basle and after we had led the division for the whole season, they once again pipped us at the post. We did reach the Swiss

Cup final against Grasshoppers Zurich, a team with a certain Christian Gross in their squad. After drawing the first game 2–2 we had to play again and on this occasion won 1–0 to lift the cup.

Halfway through the season I had been approached by the club and asked whether I was intending to stay with them and sign a further contract. I thought long and hard but basically I was frightened that my name would be forgotten in my home country and I wanted to be a coach back there. Also, all my family, most importantly my two girls, lived in England. I decided to leave. It was an enormous shame because I was still playing some great football and we had started to socialise and get to know the true Genevoise like Didi Andrey and Marc Schnyder, two of my teammates who had become close friends.

After the cup success and finishing top goalscorer in Switzerland, the press could not believe I was leaving and the players were devastated. I still have the official letter the club wrote to me on leaving which included the following line, "Everybody appreciated your intelligence, your fair play and your qualities of a first-class footballer." How is that for praise? One last story. As part of the Millennium celebrations Servette FC invited Julia and myself over to Geneva. They wanted me to be the guest of honour at the last game at their stadium before they moved to a new one in the city. It was arranged that I would fly in from the airport by helicopter and land on the centre circle with the match ball. It was an amazing trip and I was so thrilled to be thought of so highly by the directors of Servette. Julia was in the stands watching with Phil Collins, who had married a Swiss lady and was living in the area like many other superstars. We spent the afternoon together watching the game (such a nice fella). There was a banquet in the evening with many of my old teammates from the late 1970s. It was great to feel that I had made such an impact on the club.

CHAPTER FOURTEEN

THE BRIGHTON GOAL

I returned to England at the start of the 1978/79 season, and joined Norwich City for a fee of around £50,000. I am pretty sure that Martin Peters, the captain there, had put a word in for me. In pre-season, we trained near a prison in Norwich and the work we got through reflected the harsh surroundings as we ran uphill on sand. I became very fit and at the start of the season I began to score those precious goals, including one good header against Southampton in a 3–1 victory. I scored four goals in the first seven games and it looked like things were going to work out. Then disaster struck against Birmingham.

During the game I felt a sharp pain in the back of my heel. I had torn my Achilles tendon. There is not a lot of treatment you can undergo for this type of injury, except for immobilisation of the tendon, which is what we eventually went for. They were reluctant, possibly because of my age and the amount of playing time I had left, to allow me to have an operation. John Bond, the manager, asked me if I would like to try to play against Leicester in the cup. He knew full well that I was only 75 per cent fit but I said "OK" and gave it my best. But I had had an absolutely abysmal game and should have been substituted. Afterwards, Bond slated me to the press and on television saying mine was the worst performance he had ever seen from a centre forward. I thought, "Thanks! I tried to do you a favour by playing and you knew I was injured." If I was that bad why hadn't he taken me off instead of letting me suffer in agony?

The disappointment of that game was more than made up for by the birth of my second boy Luke – named after my good friend and playmate in Switzerland, Jean-Luc Martin. A couple of weeks later I went to the PFA Dinner and spoke with Alan Mullery, who was then managing Brighton. He pointed at me and said, "You are just the player I want." I shrugged my shoulders. "Sorry skip," I said, "I have got an Achilles tendon injury." His quick response was, "You'll be fine, you'll be nuisance value. Teddy Maybank, our centre forward, is banned for three games and I need someone up front." Brighton were pushing for promotion to the First Division. I knew I was finished with Norwich after Bond's unfair comments and loved the thought of playing under Mullers. He bought me for a knock-down £15,000 and off I went to the seaside.

I did no training, I just had to play those three games in place of Teddy. Even though I was limping around in every game I managed to score an instinctive header at the near post away at Leyton Orient. This proved to be an important goal, gaining a valuable point in Brighton's push for promotion. We finally achieved our goal in our last game at Newcastle, which I watched from the sidelines, and I joined in the dressing room celebrations at Mullers's insistence.

At the end of that season, the club took the whole squad and their wives to the States. San Diego, Los Angeles, Portland and Las Vegas were the wonderful places we visited. Halfway through the three-week tour I asked to return in order to have the much-needed operation on my Achilles. When you are 33 and you have had that operation it takes longer than normal to get back to any form of fitness.

The operation was a success, but after I recovered I was never strong enough, fast enough or fit enough for First Division football again. Mullers had been a very patient manager with that old body of mine and finally allowed me a free transfer. He knew of my ambitions to become a coach and allowed me to leave and try my hand with Dorchester Town FC, who had approached me.

I met with the so-called board, which included the local butcher, and they offered me a £6,000 a year salary to play and manage the team in the Southern League. Part of my many duties would include selling the advertising space around the ground and in the matchday programme. The bonus they promised for getting them into the first round proper of the FA Cup was £200, and some free sausages from the butcher. It was an impossible task to play up front and manage the team but I did my best and I did enjoy it. There were some very nice fellas in the team and it was back to grass roots football which made a refreshing change from the serious business end of football.

As time went on I found the only position I could manage from was in defence. I was certainly fit enough but it was a totally new position for me, although at that level I could get away with it. I was dealing with less talented players than I was used to so I had to be careful not to ask them to do too much tactically. I think this is one the failings of players who have reached the highest level and then discover they can't succeed as a manager. There are not many top players who have become top managers. Out of the 1966 World Cup squad only Jack Charlton became a managerial success, but think of all the other players who tried it.

One of the other obvious ones is Glenn Hoddle. He is one of the greatest players that Tottenham ever had but he hasn't been such a success as a manager. One of the things that Glenn discovered was that his players found him very intimidating because he still had all the ability to do demonstrations better then they were able to perform. In fact, he was skilful enough at the age of 14 when Ray Evans and myself went to the Harlow Schools finals to watch and present the trophies. Even then he was passing the ball accurately with the inside and outside of both feet and playing so many dummies, controlling the ball closely under pressure. I went back to Spurs and insisted that they take a look at him. I can't claim to have discovered Glenn because he was like an elephant in a haystack, as opposed to a needle, and Dick Walker, the chief scout, wasted no time in getting his signature on Tottenham forms. But I like to think I played a little part in his magnificent career as a player.

In time, Dorchester Town began to insist that I moved down to Dorset. I had managed all this time to keep my family stable in the same house in Hertfordshire. I refused to move because they only trained twice a week in the evenings and we were doing quite well with me travelling down each time. They forced my hand that Christmas and I had to resign which I did very reluctantly.

Within a week I met up with Steve Perryman at an Arsenal luncheon and he asked what I was up to and if I would be interested in going over to Norway and doing a short stint of playing 20-odd games for a Second Division team who were looking for a striker. Steve always had close ties with Norway because he had a share in some shops out there. I told him I would at least see what they had to say.

So, on New Year's Day, after a violent storm the

night before, I landed in Stavanger on the west coast of Norway to meet the chairman and vice-chairman of Vard FC in Haugesund, which is situated between Bergen and Stavanger. I thought the trip was over when I landed at four o'clock in the afternoon as it was already dark. No way. We then drove for about 45 minutes before the car was driven onto an enormous boat. Then we set off across this very rough sea having been assured that it was just a short trip.

The Bokn Fjord is notoriously dangerous and the crossing took over an hour. I began to wonder where the hell I was going and what I had let myself in for. This was a bloody long way away from home.

On the boat I was informed that Haugesund has 47,000 people and three football clubs, one of which was Vard, the club I had come to see. The gentlemen who met me spoke perfect English and in fact one looked just like a troll from the mountains of Norway. His name was Knut Tveito. They were great talkers and the more they told me about the contract the more interested I became. The season only lasted 22 games, with a break of four months in the winter due to the weather and a month's break in the summer. They were prepared to give me a two-year contract. I would have a house, a car and all flights (and boat trips) home paid for, plus a salary of £24,000. This was 1980 and that was a lot of money. I was seriously tempted because my young boys were not yet at school age and it would not be such an upheaval for them.

We decided to give it a go, so in early March 1981 we all packed up our winter woollies and departed good old England for unknown lands. During my initial trip, I had only seen the inside of a hotel in the dark. This time when we arrived in daylight it was like landing on the moon. There were rocks everywhere jutting out of the landscape, which was so barren and foreboding. Thank God the house they gave us was triple-glazed as the weather was freezing cold, wet and windy.

My first training session was a real shock. They provided us with all the football gear which included a very thick tracksuit with a hood, and some very attractive woolly tights. The training pitch was a small asphalt ground in the middle of town with six inches of snow on top. I could not believe we were being asked to train on this but somehow we did a bit of running and kicking of the ball. All Norwegians speak perfect English because the schools teach it from the age of ten, but we soon learnt that they were embarrassed to try their English except when they had a few drinks, when you could not stop them.

Because of my fear of flying, every away trip was sheer hell for me in the six-seater planes we used to get to our destinations. We had to take three of these planes to accommodate the whole squad. It was one thing I had forgotten to ask about before signing.

The pre-season pitches in March were covered in ice with banks of snow at the side and about 800 spectators. I had discarded the tights in disgust but now realised that they were a very necessary part of the kit. They were not only needed for warmth but for keeping the skin from coming off your legs when you slid on the ground.

I scored a couple of goals in the pre-season games and was looking forward to seeing a bit of grass to play on when the season began in earnest. I anticipated better football but soon discovered that the service was not as quick or as accurate as I had been used to. We had not been able to do much practice and they were not used to anyone looking to head the ball at the near post or to run onto balls over the top. After about two or three games I was offered the chance to become player/manager or player/coach because the present manager was being asked to leave. I was delighted to take over as I thought I could do a lot to bring the play up to a better standard.

We started to win a few games and we finished fifth in their league. The club and I now thought we had a good chance to go forward even though the team were all amateurs – they were firemen, bank clerks, menswear salesmen and car mechanics.

I enjoyed the Norwegian way of life. The children could run wild out there quite safely. They learnt to fish for salmon and trout, to sail boats, to ski and to play football. We also had a good time because if there is one thing the Norwegians do well it is party. Knut Tveito, the vice-chairman who looked like a troll, had taken me under his wing and introduced me to a whole gang of his mad friends who partied like crazy every weekend at their respective houses with crab, prawns, salmon and trout laid out all over their dining tables, not to mention the drink which flowed without stopping through to the early hours.

One of the first parties I went to over there with Julia was at the house of a couple called Björn and Astrid. They were in partnership with Knut. They owned boutiques together in the town. As you came into their house you were guided downstairs to the cellar for a drink. That was where the bar was. We had been there about half an hour when someone ordered us upstairs. So we walked up to the ground floor where Björn had a box of screws in his hand and Astrid had a box of nuts. The men were then told to take one of the screws and the women to take a nut. Whatever nut fitted the screw you then paired off with that woman. You were then told you had to go upstairs with your partner. I got paired with the best-looking girl at the party. Her name was Sissel and she was drop-dead gorgeous. She took my hand and she said, "Come on Martin," and she started walking me up the stairs.

I was looking back to see who Julia was with (it was Knut) but more importantly to say, "Where the hell am I being taken?" I had heard about certain Scandinavian parties and I honestly thought we going to a bedroom. Instead, Sissel walked me into a room where all the food had been laid out and where you sit down with your partner. It is their way of getting people to talk to each other. But for a moment there I thought something very different was going on. The party went on until six in the morning with a lot of music, dancing and drinking.

During the winter break, when we'd gone back home, an opportunity to take over a hotel in our village had arisen. By then, I had made the decision that I was not going to stay in football once I finished playing. I didn't want to drag my family around England from pillar to post. I had also begun to realise that my Full Coaching Badge was not a passport to a job in the football industry. We entered negotiations with the brewery to buy the hotel but at the same time Vard were offering me another year with them on top of the two I had already signed up for. The money that I could get for another year over there would certainly help us refurbish the hotel. I decided to mull it over, leaving Julia to finalise the takeover of the hotel while I returned to Norway for the new season.

We started the campaign very well and the whole town became excited about the possibility of promotion to the First Division. But I found that the problem with managing amateurs is that they have no contract and can please themselves whether they play or not. On one occasion my young goalkeeper decided three hours before a game to tell me that he was taking his girlfriend out into the country that day and would not be able to play. You can imagine the frustration and the difficulties this brought but that was their way.

Our chance of promotion came in a play-off game away to Steinkjer, north of Trondheim, managed by Bill Foulkes, the ex-Man United player. We lost the match and they got the promotion instead. I declined Vard's further offer to stay on because of the business we had just set up in England.

Just as we had done in Switzerland we had grasped the way of life in Norway with both hands and enjoyed it to the full. We still return to our friends out there to fish, party, eat and get drunk. My boys and I still fish the rivers with Knut to this day.

It all happened so suddenly. I was no longer a professional footballer, although to be honest I did not get much time to think about it. Everything comes to an end but I have to confess that for the first couple of years of my retirement whenever I watched Spurs I always felt I could still have done it. I had played professional football for 20 years and knew nothing else. Looking back the good times always outweighed the bad. I have always been disappointed that my boys came along too late and never saw me play. In fact my eldest boy Nick, at the age of 11, enquired whether I had ever played in front of 10,000 people. He had no idea that I had played at Wembley in front of 100,000.

CHAPTER FIFTEEN

THE NEW FAWLTY TOWERS

With my football days over, I fully took over the running of the Brookmans Park Hotel on my return from Norway in 1982. To open the hotel I asked if Bill would kindly do the honours: and he accepted. For the ceremony 2,000 people from the village showed up and mingled with the likes of Bobby Moore, Glenn Hoddle, Stevie Perryman, Phil Beal and Ralph Coates. For the first few years, it was like Fawlty Towers. We certainly could have given John Cleese a few ideas if he had asked. We had 13 people working behind the bar when normally three would have done and the village had never known anything like it. Pity it didn't continue that way.

There was the time when an old lady guest locked herself in the bathroom only to find the key when I was halfway up a ladder outside the building. Or the young white-suited and gloved health-and-safety students who pounced with relish on the tin of chestnut purée they found at the back of chef's larder labelled 1971. Or the massive black rat that only our barman Roger and I saw as it weaved its way across the floor of a crowded bar. And that unforgettable smell of Glade Fern air freshener which Roger sprayed liberally and unsubtly around the bar to try to disguise that unmistakable smell of rotting rat as the little blue granules left by the pest man claimed another victim somewhere in the depths of the building. Fortunately, we never did have anyone die on us, even though we served kippers for breakfast.

Julia and I took over a business with lettuces growing out of our ears we were so green and became known to our customers as Basil and Sybil. Our biggest problem in those early days was that we trusted everyone. We had alcoholic chefs brandishing knives, bar staff stealing money and bar cellar managers pilfering bottles. Thank God we had a good accountant and a great stock-taker who taught us all the tricks of the trade and set us straight.

We did not have to live on the premises as we were only 800 yards up the road which was a luxury with young children. The hotel was a big, beautiful building but it was a sponge for money. We started with just the bar and a bar food area that we extended to serving Sunday lunch. After a year we realised the big potential for the hotel was in the banqueting suite which had not been used for many years. So we decorated it and started hosting weddings, dinner dances and functions.

Finally the derelict hotel rooms were refurbished and they became our bread-and-butter trade. I hadn't worked nearly as hard as this when I was in football. It was 24 hours a day, seven days a week but it was so satisfying to succeed in another occupation. Julia and I worked all hours; we were never a couple who just stood around propping up the front of the bar. And the hotel provided us with many laughs and stories that we treasure.

I pulled pints along with my staff and was constantly up on the roof mending holes in the asphalt with a big pan of bitumen on the cooker while Saturday lunch was being served. I cut the lawns and polished the enormous hall and banqueting hall floors. Julia turned her hand to every aspect of the hotel: making beds when the chambermaid disappeared, cooking for a hundred when the chef was drunk, silver-service waitressing and cleaning out the loos after the drunks had been sick.

After several years we finally amassed the most wonderful reliable team of staff and we became one big family who worked hard but enjoyed each other and most importantly were able to laugh a lot of the time.

We even had three football teams made up of the hotel's staff, customers and boys living around the area. We played in the St Albans league, and I played in the first team for many years. We won the league one year and Bill Nick presented the trophy. Our home pitch was at the Royal Veterinary grounds, and after every match we would go back to the hotel and have a drink. Eventually both my sons were big and strong enough to play with me on Sunday mornings for the team. That was a great thrill, to be on the same football field with them. They could get very overprotective towards me, though. On one occasion I was fouled and went tumbling over with my opponent ending up on top of me. Nick and Luke raced across ready to sort this guy out, only for me to tell them I was fine, before holding him down and giving him a good whack myself.

I was behind the bar one day and one of the opposing players' girlfriends said, "Are you Martin Chivers?" I said, "Yes." She said, "My mum named her dog after you," and one of my players said, "That's a bit cruel, fancy calling a dog Slow Bastard." I've had so many people over the years come up and say they named their dog or cat after me.

One lunchtime I was really pleasantly surprised to see Alan Gilzean and his two sons walk into the bar. Gilzean had moved into Potters Bar for a while and you can imagine how we reminisced. It is sad to say that I have not seen him since, especially after all the escapades. Top players like Mike Summerbee and Alan Brazil have since stated that the best striking partnership at Spurs in their opinion was mine and Gilly's.

Eighteen years was a long time in the licensed trade. Julia was the driving force in our hotel business. Her ability to keep a stressful business such as ours together along with raising two boys is just incredible. I just hope she thinks it has all been worth it. We both missed a lot of time with our two boys in their early years and had to employ Norwegian au pairs to help out. One of them came back and visited when Nick and Luke were coming towards the end of their school-days. Much to both of their amazement, she now looked like Miss World. When I told the boys that she used to bath them their jaws dropped. It left us exhausted and we realised we were not as young as we used to be. The hotel needed an injection of finance and ideas to give it a new lease of life. We had neither and as we were burnt out we were very glad to step aside in September 1999 and let someone else take over.

I have a private football pension of £35 per week and certainly needed a job when we finished with the hotel. I have been working ever since, not only at Tottenham in the hospitality suites but also in the construction business with the grand title of Business Development Manager in asbestos consultancy.

When Mike Rollo at Tottenham offered me the position of matchday host at the club in 1990, I was confident that I could do it. I had been rather shy to start with at the hotel, not eager to put myself forward in any way, and all the toastmastering at the weddings was done by my wife. But it became increasingly obvious they wanted a man to officiate. In time, I was able to stand up in front of 140 guests in the suite and do all the necessary announcements and direct the ceremony. That gave me my apprenticeship in public speaking.

Having said that, to be honest I have never been afraid to stand up in front of the fans at Tottenham because I consider White Hart Lane to be my second home. You have to be diplomatic and can't run the club down in any way or criticise the manager, the players, the tactics or their performance on the day.

I remember going to Udinese for a UEFA Cup trip at the start of the 2008/09 season when we were at the bottom of the league and struggling badly. I told the 30 VIP travelling supporters, "I know enough about football to know there is something very wrong but I can't tell you what. All I can say is just be patient, just one good game can change our luck and give the players the confidence that they are screaming out for." That was my way of telling them that things would change one way or another. Soon after, Juande Ramos left.

Over the 19 years I have been watching and working at Spurs, I have obviously seen good and bad times. I have seen 13 managers come and go which, in my experience, is not conducive to continued success. I have learnt that the most important people are the fans and I consider myself one of them now. In my playing days I had a bad reputation of being standoffish to the fans and declined many autographs but now, working at Spurs, I have had the opportunity of making amends and have all the time in the world for them. I am very grateful to be recognised. It will be a very sad day when

I am not stopped on the street and chatted to about the old times.

I enjoy every Saturday home game and have worked the Legends Lounge, the Bill Nicholson Suite and the Oak Room. The most important thing I learnt in the hotel business is that you are only as good as your staff. The boys and girls who work at Spurs are great at their job and good company.

We have an unusually large nucleus of Spurs legends hosting the various lounges on matchdays. Martin Peters, Pat Jennings, Ralph Coates, Cliff Jones, Phil Beal, John Pratt, Alan Mullery, Paul Allen and, of course, myself. No club will ever get quality players like these to work for them in the future because it does not pay to be loyal now. A move between clubs makes money and increased wages which gives them security for the rest of their lives. We were one big family when we were players and are all pleased to be able to see each other on a regular basis.

Some of us never actually hung up our football boots because 20 years ago or more I started to organise an ex-Spurs football team to play at charity and fundraising events all over the country. There has even been demand for us to go abroad and we played a match before Spurs against Lyn Oslo in a pre-season friendly on 25th July 1993. My teammates were Peter Shreeve, John Pratt, Mark Falco, Garry Brooke, Tony Galvin, Phil Beal, Ralph Coates and Ray Clemence in goal. We won 4–3 and I managed to get off the ground and score the winner with my head. The players were real stalwarts to turn up on rainy days in front of a few hundred people with their aches and pains and bad knees due for operations, all shapes and sizes now, ready to perform yet again. And believe me they could give any team a bloody good game.

Truth is we were all still thrilled to put on that Spurs shirt and try to turn the clock back to more agile and pacier times.

Naturally, people ask me about the game today and the money the players earn. You'd be lying if you said you weren't envious. The sad thing about football is it used to be the working man's sport and it is not now. A large part of the revenue is business and corporate hospitality, as it is with so many sports. If a father wants to take his two children along to see a game it costs an arm and a leg. Despite that we still have 20,000 names on a waiting list for season tickets to watch Tottenham. But then we are the finest team the world has ever seen.

My three best friends all came from my football days. I met Clive Bednash, a big Spurs fan, in my early days at Tottenham when many players would meet up at his club Room At The Top in Ilford. I spent many an evening there with Bobby Moore and some of his teammates. He has remained a great friend to this day. In Switzerland I met Ray Lewis who is godfather to my son Luke and we still spend time together in each other's country. All my children go skiing in Switzerland with Julia and I trailing behind. My old fishing buddy and Norwegian troll is Knut Tveito and, as I have mentioned, my boys and I still fish together in the fjords. My four children are my greatest joy in life and now I am a proud grandfather to four boys, almost a football team, with more to come I hope.

My wife Julia has always been a horse rider and likens professional footballers to thoroughbred race horses. Most of them need gelding! When they take the mickey or are too full of themselves, they need a jag in the mouth. When they are stubborn or are napping, they need a kick in the ribs with spurs or a sharp whack with a whip. When they are nervous or unsure they get a calm, soothing voice and an encouraging gentle pat on the neck. They shoot old horses but the death throes of an ageing footballer are played out in public as he progresses down the divisions, fighting ever-increasing injuries, still believing that he has something to offer on the football field, never wanting to hang up his boots. Some, if they have the right attitude and temperament, can be retrained in another discipline and go on to have productive, useful lives and make a good companion for someone for the rest of their time. I hope that's me. And I hope that despite receiving a few yellow cards in our time together she doesn't regret persevering with married life to a goal obsessed footballer.

Also, isn't it funny how in life so much changes but stays the same? Take me. Tonight I will go to sleep and dream about scoring the perfect goal. I have done that all my life. I did that when I was a kid in Southampton kicking a tennis ball against a wall and I still do it today. In my dreams I score goals for Tottenham and I score goals for England although sometimes the dream winds you up because you just can't get the ball in the back of the net. Other dreams you score the best goals of your life and you wake up feeling great.

POSTCRIPT

THE LIGHTS GO OUT IN HIS OFFICE

There is one more tale to tell.

Towards the end of my time at Servette, a Spurs youth team accompanied by Bill Nicholson came over to play in a tournament in Geneva. Bill had come with his wife Darkie to visit his daughter Linda and her husband. I went over to the hotel and met up with Bill and the young players. I was very apprehensive about how Bill would be with me, especially after all the rumours that I had been one of the reasons that he resigned as Spurs manager. I found Bill in the hotel restaurant as the players were having breakfast. We greeted each other and I sat down with him. It was a very easy going chat with no animosity at all. I went home and told Julia this. She replied, "Why don't you ask him out to dinner?" My response was immediate. "What Bill Nicholson? You must be joking."

But Julia was insistent. "It would be the best thing you could ever do," she said. That evening I phoned him and invited the Nicholson family to dinner. To my utter surprise he accepted. I was absolutely sure he would turn down the invitation.

We decided to take him and Darkie to the Pavillion du Ruth which is a famous restaurant on the side of Lake Geneva. Their specialty was filet de perch from the lake. Fish and chips to Bill. We met there and went to our table together. I was very apprehensive but to my great relief the conversation flowed. We didn't talk about the football much – more about life in general, families, that kind of stuff. I found him to be a delightful man. He was very relaxed and great company. He showed a side of himself I had never seen before. In fact I found out later that Darkie had said to Bill after we parted, "Is that the same Martin Chivers, the same player who drove you mad all those years ago at Tottenham? I found him to be a complete gentleman."

When I got back to England after my various travels, I began to bump into Bill at the Tottenham training ground. Not a word was ever said about the past – I had too much respect for the man to bring up old wounds or battles. Besides, I think I had changed. I was more relaxed, more diplomatic too, and our relationship got better and better. We always reminisced about the good times and every time I met him, I could tell by his smile how pleased he was when he saw me coming. It was a smile I never experienced in the days when I was playing under him.

In hindsight I can understand the frustrations that Bill and Eddie experienced watching me play. To this day I refuse to watch DVD's of my old games. Even though it was proved that I was the fastest runner at Spurs, it certainly never looks like it on film. I look so lethargic. Bill and Edie's constant criticism of me was therefore designed to push me a little bit more. It certainly worked in that Wolves game and many others as well. Today, I truly think that it was a real shame we didn't get to know each other better at Spurs. If I am honest I think the real problem is that we were both stubborn. We never sat down and tried to iron out our differences. I know Bill once said that I never reached my true potential and this was obviously the source of much frustration for him. Who knows what sort of player I would have been if that aggression that Bill yearned for had been part of my make up?

Yet when I look back at my time with Spurs I just think it was wonderful. We were a family: the team, the management and especially the fans. You see, the crowd counteracted so much of Bill's criticisms. Going up that tunnel and then, boom, walking into that noise, all those people singing your name, it was fantastic. With them behind me, I could not put a foot wrong. I wanted to take every Spurs fan to every away game cause they gave me all the confidence in the world.

In 1990, when I began to do some hospitality for

Tottenham at home games, my main jobs were to look after the people in the 36 boxes they had built in the new East Stand and host the Legend's Lounge.

Bill had also started to attend games again and would sit in the Legend's Lounge to watch the match. It was perfect for him as he could park his car nearby, see the game and leave ten minutes before the end to get home without any bother. I am sure he could have sat in the director's box but he hated to make a fuss and I think he had become a little embarrassed by his physical difficulties. He once told me that he felt his legs weren't his any more. Another reason he stayed in the East Stand was so as not to not draw attention to himself leaving the director's box ten minutes before the end of the game. That wouldn't have done. Even when my other old manager, Ted Bates, came to visit with Southampton, Bill could not be persuaded to come and meet with him in the director's box. Ted himself was not capable of getting across the East Stand and although they were dying to meet each other, the two old men never got to shake hands again. I found this so frustrating that they were so close in distance but could not make the final 300 yards. All I could do was convey their best regards to each other.

At half time in every home game, I would bring Bill out a cup of tea and discuss what we had seen. He might have been a bit wobbly on his legs but he still had all his marbles and a memory like an elephant. He would always speak his mind. "Bloody centre forward, there's no movement, he's not putting himself about." On another occasion I heard him muttering, "Bloody Sheringham. He's meant to be a good player, he's not doing a thing." I thought, "You haven't changed, have you Bill." Teddy should have had Bill as his manager and experienced some of the stick I got. Bill was very critical about all the new players the club signed and I loved to listen to him holding court on football matters.

As the years went by, I found there was a lot more to the man than the one I barely spoke to as a player. Even though he still lived in Tottenham he loved his allotment and planting his vegetables and flowers. I invited him round my house in Brookmans Park for dinner one night and he and Darkie drove all the way from Creighton Road in Tottenham. We also invited Morris Keston, Ralph Coates (Darkie's favourite), Phil Beal and Bill's daughter Jean and her husband Colin, who lived nearby. I wanted to make it an evening where we could talk about the old times. It worked perfectly. I'd never seen him so relaxed and that's when I realised Bill did like a glass of red wine. He drank a good half a bottle that night and then drove himself home.

When I celebrated my 50th birthday in my hotel with about a hundred people, I invited friends from home and abroad, including many ex-players such as Steve Perryman, Pat Jennings and Joe Kinnear. The special guest was Bill Nicholson with his wife Darkie, who gave me a stone cockerel as a present, which still stands proudly in my garden to this day. Bill stayed the whole evening talking to everyone and making friends with my sons.

There was a big campaign at the time to get him a knighthood, which I feel was only right and proper. I know he got a CBE but let's face it, there are younger sportsmen out there who have received that honour but not given 60 years of service to football. He was the first manager to win the league and cup Double and the first English manager to win a European trophy. Spurs had already given him one testimonial but once they confirmed there was going to be another in 2002, his daughter Jean was immediately on the phone to me. She asked me if I would look after her dad during the testimonial. I said I'd be thrilled and honoured.

The game was a pre-season fixture against Fiorentina in front of a full house. In the tunnel, I stood with Bill, and the then Spurs manager Glenn Hoddle and all of us were in a great mood. As we waited to walk out onto the pitch we kept smiling and joking. It was a lovely five minutes. When the time came I asked Bill if he would like to walk out without his walking stick. "As long as you keep hold of me," he replied, as he was now very unsteady on his feet. I knew he was a very proud man and I knew the walking stick was an embarrassment for him. We followed the teams out, then they formed a guard of honour and he shook hands with each player to a wondrous applause from the fans. I was increasingly aware of his tightening grip on my right arm but I held him steady. We were asked to go to the centre circle and to wave to all four corners of the ground. I said, "Bill, don't rush this, enjoy it."

He waved to the east, north, west and then we tottered round to face the south when he suddenly decided to milk the tremendous applause and use both hands to wave. My immediately reaction was to focus only on him and sure enough, he swayed backwards. Thankfully I managed to grab hold of his arm and hold him up upright. Nobody seemed to notice. He got a standing ovation that seemed to last for ever and he really enjoyed it, smiling all the time. He had drummed into everyone while he was manager – the players, the staff, the office, everyone who worked in the club – that the fans were the most important people. Because of that he got the sort of reception from them that no other person could get. I was so moved for him.

He and Darkie moved to Potters Bar to be near his daughter and I saw even more of him, including one occasion at Barbara Wallace's birthday party on a boat on the River Lea. Barbara was a great character at Tottenham and ran Bill's office with a smile and a rod of iron. She was the most diplomatic of women, handling with ease all the demands and tantrums that must have gone on at the club.

Bill suffered greatly with his legs and circulation problems and eventually he had to be admitted to the Potters Bar hospital. Having gained permission, I went in to see him a couple of times and took him a bottle of good red wine left over from my daughter Melanie's wedding. On enquiring whether he was allowed such a thing the response from the head nurse was, "Oh yes, Bill's allowed red wine; he loves it, doesn't he?" The best we could do was a couple of plastic beakers but we still managed to work our way through the bottle. I asked if the wine was OK and his response was, "It's not as good as I normally drink but it will do." Cheeky bugger. It had cost me a fortune. That was the last time I saw him.

Bill Nicholson died on 23rd October 2004. Jean phoned us that evening and we were devastated. I was planning on going in to see him again and now I couldn't. It was so upsetting. I had known that man for 36 years.

On 7th November Tottenham laid on a memorial service for him and it was fantastic. They set it all up at the Paxton Road end. They decorated the ground, held a service on the pitch and at the end of it they let 85 white doves into the air to represent every year of Bill's life. The club asked certain players to say a few words and I was so thrilled to be one of them. Jimmy Greaves and Cliffy Jones went first and they were very funny. Then there was Stevie Perryman and then myself, Glenn Hoddle and Gary Mabbutt. By the end of my speech I was choked up. To say something nice about someone who has passed away I find very very hard to do. To say something about this man was nearly impossible. Bill Nicholson was a second father figure to me. I look at photographs of us together and I think, "You are just like my dad, a man who was as honest as they come." Like my father, Bill didn't have a lot of humour but he could still make me laugh like no other. I remember him showing me holiday photos from Scarborough and the whole family were wearing overcoats and had scarves wrapped round their necks, freezing their backsides off in the wind and the rain. He took my ribbing about it very well and could at last, it seemed, laugh at himself.

At that memorial service I said the one thing about Bill I will never forget is that he always said the fans were the most important people at Tottenham. He said that to every player who came under him and he was right. When I work in the Bill Nicholson Suite I always make a point of telling the people in there, "Right now you are in the great man's lounge and that he always said that you, the fans, are the most important thing about this club." And I am not the only one to do so. All the players working in those lounges tell the same story.

Bill Nicholson and I didn't see eye to eye as player and manager but after that night in that restaurant in Geneva, we developed a relationship that remains one of the most significant of my life. Julia was right. Inviting him out for dinner that night in Switzerland was the best thing I ever did.

MARTIN CHIVERS'S SPEECH AT BILL NICHOLSON'S MEMORIAL SERVICE, 7th November 2004

Good morning everybody.

I am very honoured to speak on behalf of the '70s players in celebration of Bill's life. We all called him Bill because he didn't like the term 'Boss'. The team of the '70s really was one big happy family and believe it or not eight members of that family are still involved here at White Hart Lane.

Bill's professionalism and passion for football and Spurs meant that after every game he would immediately start thinking of the next one and the lights would be burning in his office until all hours that same evening. With that work ethos and that passion goes perfection, and he demanded that from every player – as I should know to my cost.

His integrity in all his dealings with his players both on and off the pitch was unquestionable. There was no hand of influence on him. His forthright honesty led him into the Wolves dressing room after the game here in 1972 to commiserate with them on being the better team, while we waited for him to drink champagne from the UEFA Cup which we had just won.

Despite his position at the club, Bill was the sort of person who would talk to everyone: from the directors to the security men, to the fans, to the ladies who washed the kit, he gave time to them all.

He considered Spurs fans so loyal that they deserved the very best. Our trust and confidence in his ability and tactics inspired us to four major finals in four years.

Everyone knew he lived just down the road and in recent years he hardly missed a game, sitting in his Legends seat in the East Stand and more recently in the directors' box.

His fame did not change him, he regarded his job as the best in the world and if he is looking down on us today he would genuinely be surprised at all the fuss, as he always was when honoured or singled out in any way.

Thank you.

FINAL QUESTIONS

Fans can come out with some amazing questions and stories always beginning with, "Do you remember me? I was the fan who ran on the field after the League Cup final and gave you a scarf to wave." Or the guy who spoke with me at Tottenham recently in front of his friends and said, "I ran onto the field after the final whistle and asked you for your autograph and I bet you don't know what you said." I replied "I probably told you to piss off." "Exactly" he said in surprise.

People ask me so many questions that I thought if I have not covered them all in this book I would do so right at the end. So here goes.

What was your best goal?
Without doubt the second goal against Wolves in the UEFA Cup final.

What was your most satisfying goal?
That's easy. I actually got off the ground at 63 years of age and headed a cross from my son Nick into the goal in the last charity game I played in. Son to father, father to goal, magic.

Who was your toughest opponent?
The 1970 Leeds team – the whole lot. However Ron Yeats really hurt me the most when I was carried off after one of his 'tackles'.

Who was the best player you ever played with?
My whole Spurs team of the early '70s. They all had different positions and were all brilliant at what they did.

Do you watch old videos of your games?
No, I can't watch myself playing as I looked so slow. It is frustrating.

How did you celebrate scoring a goal?
I certainly never thought of taking off my shirt and throwing it into the crowd because it was the only one you were given to last the whole season.

What was your biggest disappointment?
The World Cup qualifier against Poland.

What was your greatest moment?
I've been lucky, I've got too many to choose from.

Who is your favourite team apart from Tottenham?
Without doubt Barcelona because I just love their football.

And here is one from one of my sons – Did you ever swerve the ball like Ronaldo?
Swerve it? We had enough trouble getting the ball off the ground it was so heavy.

MARTIN CHIVERS CAREER STATISTICS

CLUB CAREER

SOUTHAMPTON (1961–1968)

League appearances – 175
League goals – 96
Cup appearances – 15
Cup goals – 10

TOTTENHAM HOTSPUR (1968–1976)

League appearances – 268
League goals – 118
Cup appearances – 87
Cup goals – 56

Martin also set two records at Spurs by scoring 22 goals in 32 UEFA Cup games and 23 goals in 33 League Cup games. These records are yet to beaten and will probably remain intact throughout his lifetime, a fact that gives him immense pleasure. He also grabbed 11 goals in 22 FA Cup games.

SERVETTE (1976–1978)

League appearances – 64

Goals – 36

NORWICH CITY (1978–1979)

League appearances –11

Goals – 4

BRIGHTON & HOVE ALBION (1979–1980)

League appearances – 5

Goals – 1

INTERNATIONAL CAREER

ENGLAND (1971–1973)

Appearances – 24

Goals – 13